The Price of Politics: Lessons from *Kelo v. City of New London*

The Price of Politics: Lessons from *Kelo v. City of New London*

Kyle Scott

ROWMAN & LITTLEFIELD EDUCATION

A division of

ROWMAN & LITTLEFIELD PUBLISHERS, INC.
Lanham • New York • Toronto • Plymouth, UK

Published by Lexington Books
A division of Rowman & Littlefield Publishers, Inc.
A wholly owned subsidiary of The Rowman & Littlefield Publishing Group, Inc.
4501 Forbes Boulevard, Suite 200, Lanham, Maryland 20706
http://www.lexingtonbooks.com

Estover Road, Plymouth PL6 7PY, United Kingdom

British Library Cataloguing in Publication Information Available

Scott, Kyle, 1977–
    The price of politics : lessons from Kelo v. City of New London / Kyle Scott.
        p. cm.
    Includes bibliographical references and index.
    ISBN 978-0-7391-3383-5 (cloth : alk. paper)—ISBN 978-0-7391-3384-2 (pbk. : alk.
paper) — ISBN 978-0-7391-3385-9 (electronic)
    1. Eminent domain—United States.   2. Human rights—United States.   3. Eminent
domain—Connecticut—New London—Cases.   4. Kelo, Susette—Trials, litigation,
etc.   5. New London (Conn.)—Trials, litigation, etc.   I. Title.
    KF5599.S36 2009
    343.73'0252—dc22   2009032234

Printed in the United States of America

⊚™ The paper used in this publication meets the minimum requirements of American
National Standard for Information Sciences—Permanence of Paper for Printed Library
Materials, ANSI/NISO Z39.48-1992

Printed in the United States of America.

Contents

Acknowledgments

During the year it took to write this book, I received unprecedented support and encouragement from my colleagues at the University of North Florida. Matthew Corrigan did a tremendous job encouraging me and keeping me insulated from administrative tasks, even while he was feeling his way through his first year as chair, which made the completion of this book possible. Darren Wheeler, who was completing his own book at the time, proved to be a valuable resource during the process.

Outside of the department, I received helpful comments from Michael Zuckert who read an earlier draft of one of the chapters. Also, the comments from the participants—particularly Teena Wilhelm at the 2008 Southern Political Science Association annual meeting—were quite informative.

My friend Justin Allen contributed in many ways. Most importantly, he reminded me that some of the best ideas occur outside of academic circles.

I have now worked with Joseph Parry on two books. It has been a pleasure in each instance, and I hope to work with him in the future.

Chapter 2 of this book, like all of my thinking on politics in some way or another, was inspired by the teaching of the late Ross Lence. It is almost an injustice to credit him as he would have done a much better job writing this book. While his ideas have informed mine, I am so far removed from his grasp of politics and the great books that I can only hope he will excuse my efforts.

Finally, to my brilliant and beautiful wife, Bethany, and our two brilliant and beautiful children, Braden and Berkeley. It is your patience, joy, and love that made this work possible and give it meaning.

List of Tables

Introduction

For the most part, Supreme Court decisions fly under the public's radar, but the 2005 Supreme Court decision of *Kelo v. City of New London* captured everyone's attention. The reaction was in response to the Court's curtailment of individual property rights. People feel strongly about their rights, especially their property rights. A public statement by Connecticut's Governor M. Jodi Rell is indicative of the public response: "This issue is the twenty-first century equivalent of the Boston Tea Party: the government taking away the rights and liberties of property owners without giving them a voice. But this time it is not a monarch wearing robes in England we are fighting—but five robed justices at the Supreme Court" (Rell 2005). The immediate questions are: Why are people so attached to their property rights? And, should they be?

Property has a dual value: intrinsic and instrumental. Intrinsic values are those that are good in and of themselves. Instrumental values are those values that can lead to outcomes consistent with intrinsic values. Most rights have only intrinsic or instrumental value: property has both. Property has an intrinsic value because people naturally think in terms of what belongs to them and what belongs to others. The desire to acquire and to secure possessions is a basic human characteristic—for better or worse—that cannot be ignored. Therefore, property rights protect a part of humanity that is natural to its existence. Property has an instrumental value in that it helps guarantee other rights and leads to economic development. Countries with secure property rights achieve greater economic prosperity and also see the successful protection of other rights. Property is regarded as a basic human right by Americans, a sentiment that can be traced to the earliest colonies. Property is essential to one's existence, independence, and happiness. "Without property, real and personal, one could not enjoy life and liberty, and could not

xi

be free and independent" (Levy 1995, p. 18). This was the understanding of property during the founding era, and it still exists among many in the general public. Aside from the moral considerations of property, there are also legal and historical considerations that derive from the moral considerations. "Americans consider property a constitutionally protected right and saw the Court taking away that right. "

This book argues that the Court's decision was wrong. The Court's reading of the Constitution and the nation's legal heritage was flawed. The majority in *Kelo* suffers from a faulty jurisprudence. The primary consideration in the Court's decision was the social effect of the property seizure. Such utilitarian pragmatism[1] has no place in Supreme Court decisions. Judges should be constrained by the law and Constitution; elected officials are the only ones who can be excused for utilitarian pragmatism. Once judges begin acting like legislators, they will upset the delicate balance Alexander Hamilton described in *Federalist* #78. In looking to uncover the meaning of the Constitution, judges should read the text literally, and if there is still uncertainty, they should consult those who drafted and ratified the document by exploring primary documents from the era as well as the legal and political philosophies that influenced the authors of those documents. Certainly the Constitution can err, and when it does, it ought to be corrected. This is the job of the people and their elected representatives. The Court interprets what the document says; it should not have the power to amend it.

Undoubtedly, there will be criticism of my method of constitutional interpretation. Those who go to the original sources are characterized as *originalists* and criticized as such.[2] I can hardly understand why this is a criticism, as even those who are not originalists go back to the Constitution and debate what it says. The only people worthy of derogatory references are those who say that the Constitution has no bearing on the interpretation of the Constitution. Those who take the document seriously as a binding force on modern politics ought to be congratulated. Some people advocate a departure from the Constitution and advocate a new reading of it; this does not preclude the position of the originalists but instead advocates a move away from the original document. These revisionists simply state that the original reading does not meet modern needs, but they do not refute the original reading or the originalists' methodology.

For example, Bruce Ackerman's defense of the unconventional method of amending the Constitution during Civil War Reconstruction does not deny the originalist position. He simply holds that the original intention, the most literal interpretation, of Article V should not have bound Reconstruction era politics. This does not deny an originalist reading of Article V. All it says is that such a reading ought not to be binding because of the unique conditions lawmakers confronted during Reconstruction. Such a position is ultimately unpalatable as it advocates lawlessness and relativism, which is why Ackerman, too, slips into a form of originalism as he defends his position on the grounds that American history has often seen unconventional methods of lawmaking. According to Ackerman, unconventional lawmaking is consistent with the original intention of the founders. Simply put, according to Ackerman, the Reconstruction interpretation and violation of Article V is no different than what was done when the U.S. Constitution was drafted or when the colonists declared their independence. Thus, in practice, even Ackerman is an originalist.

Very few constitutional scholars make arguments that do not directly draw upon the Constitution. The question is, What does the document say and how do we settle a dispute over interpretation when one arises? My position is that one should consider the historical, legal, and philosophical influences of those who penned the words of the document under consideration. Still, some disagree with this position, but I think it has less to do with the method and more to do with the ideology that usually accompanies the method.

Originalists are typically aligned with conservative viewpoints, which is also true of advocates of economic liberties. In this book, I employ—and therefore tacitly defend—the originalist methodology, while not aligning myself with all of its proponents and practitioners. If nothing else, this book is a call to bridge the ideological gap on matters of constitutional interpretative methodology. The first step is to suggest that one should not reject the originalist position because one does not like the politics of those who call themselves originalists, but rather confront the methodology on its merits.

The argument over originalism parallels the central concern for this book: property rights. Property rights are not rights for the rich or for the conservative. Property rights are fundamental for the preservation of all other rights. In this book, I seek to show that there is a unity of rights, and that rights should not be an ideologically divisive issue, on the grounds that the principles underlying all constitutionally protected rights are the same. While people may disagree about what rights should be promoted and to what extent, there should be some agreement that all constitutionally protected rights are important for everyone. Throughout this book I will show how government infringement on property rights is not just economically damaging but damaging to all other rights without resorting to slippery-slope arguments. I do this by drawing on the thought of those thinkers who informed the thought of the revolutionary and founding generation to show that all of the rights in the Bill of Rights are derived from the same source and rest on the same principle.

My view of the Constitution and the rights contained therein dictates how I will discuss the subject. By taking the position that the Constitution is the ultimate authority on what the Constitution says, I do not find it necessary to partake in the usual practice of providing a history of all case law pertaining to the subject matter at hand. While useful in some books, in this one it would be merely pedantic. This book does not provide a history of case law as I am more interested in uncovering the discrepancy between our era and the founders' era than in tracking the ebb and flow of judicial decisions. This book argues that in *Kelo* there has been a departure from the original meaning of the Constitution. Rather than simply trace the Court's decisions on the question of property rights and decide whether *Kelo* is consistent or inconsistent with these decisions, this book argues that the decision is inconsistent with the original meaning of the Constitution and investigates the implications, meaning, and potential reasons for the departure.

The question may then be raised, How can one decide if a case is consistent with the Constitution without relying on other cases? My methodology for Constitutional interpretation does not require an extensive treatment of precedent or legislative action. While one certainly cannot ignore previous decisions, one should not be bound by them in interpreting the Constitution. When interpreting the Constitution, we should first understand for ourselves what the Constitution says and then look at the cases to see if they are consistent or inconsistent with the Constitution. This requires one to embark on a first reading of sorts. Cases should not cloud our vision of the Constitution. We should look to the Constitution for its meaning, rather than to the Court.

I prefer the Constitution to precedents because precedents can rest on shaky ground. When we recognize that judges are not above error or bias then it becomes clear that a decision can be an incorrect reading of the Constitution. Imagine that a decision (D_1) is made that comes close to, but does not fully achieve, a correct reading of the Constitution as it applies to the matter in question. Now, if D_1 is used by a later Court to interpret the Constitution, then D_2 will have moved one step away from the Constitution because it sees the Constitution through the lens of D_1. It is easy to imagine how far away from the Constitution we get when we reach D_{20} or D_{30}. Whereas some decisions may move us closer to the Constitution, even if they build upon previous decisions, they will never get us to the Constitution, and the general trend will always be a move away from the Constitution.

My view of the development of judicial precedent is an applied version of Plato's Forms as discussed in Book X of the *Republic*. Plato states that there is an ideal table (as there is an ideal for everything), and the carpenter makes a table that approximates the ideal but does not achieve it. There is a painting based upon the carpenter's rendering of a table, which is further removed from the true table than the carpenter's version. Those who see the painting or make poems about tables based upon the painting are even further removed from the true table. Such is the case with some Constitutional doctrines. I do not argue that the Constitution is the true form of justice, only that it is the true form of the Constitution and everything else is merely an interpretation.

So while I may argue for a reading of the Constitution that the Court has never articulated as a controlling standard, I have no qualms with departing from the Court's reading of the Constitution or arguing for a position that the Court never has, because it is the Constitution I look to, and not the Court, when seeking what is constitutional. I certainly admit that the Constitution can err, and where it does it ought to be corrected through the proper channels. But this book argues that on the question of property, the Constitution with the Bill of Rights properly conceives of property and its place within the community, economics, and politics.

This book is composed of seven chapters. Each chapter can stand on its own because each chapter addresses a different dimension of the property debate. But, each successive chapter does build upon the previous. This is particularly important for the more subtle aspects of my argument. For instance, in reading the state constitutions, I read *ought* as binding rather than suggestive. The reader will not understand why this is the case unless my reading of the common law tradition and John Locke—and their respective influence on the colonies and state constitutions—in the previous chapters has been understood and carried over.

Chapter 1 will show that the legal and historical origins of property rights can be traced to the common law. By discussing property rights in England, the chapter serves as a foundation for later discussions of why property rights are important in the United States. This chapter shows the historic and legal origin of property and due process rights as well as the intrinsic and instrumental value of these rights.

Chapter 2 provides an analysis of John Locke's thought on property. By focusing on the *Second Treatise*, I will discuss Locke's understanding of property and its connection to his political theory. Chapters 3 and 4 will refer back to this chapter in order to demonstrate Locke's influence on the nation's founding and the centrality of property in both Locke's thought and in the U.S. Constitution. This chapter provides a philosophical justification for property rights and continues to discuss the intrinsic and instrumental value of property rights and their relation to due process rights.

Much of the legal history written on the American founding ignores the legal culture of the colonies. Chapter 3 seeks to help rectify this deficiency in political science literature. The colonies had their own constitutions and laws before the U.S. Constitution was written. In order to gain a clear understanding of what the Constitution meant by *property,* I will look to the constitutions, charters, and laws that preceded the U.S. Constitution. I will focus primarily on the constitutions of the colonies and the Northwest Ordinance. This chapter will link the historical and philosophical origins of rights in England to the development of rights in America.

Next, I will focus on the ratification of the Bill of Rights and postrevolutionary American thought. While there were other important figures in the founding era, it was James Madison who made the strongest argument for the protection of property rights. And because it was Madison who drafted the Bill of Rights in which the protection of private property was codified, it is important to understand Madison's thought on the matter. I will demonstrate the close parallel between Locke and Madison in addition to a discussion of how Madison's ideas should inform our interpretation of the Constitution and Bill of Rights.

Chapter 5 deals with the three eminent domain cases decided by the Supreme Court in the 2004–2005 term. In discussing each of the cases, I will test the logic used by the justices in the opinion, critically examine each case's use of case law, and draw out instances in which the Court departed from the original meaning of the Constitution. I focus primarily on those cases that are referred to in the opinions and do not give a general survey of eminent domain case law, for the reasons described earlier. It is only necessary to show that there has been a departure from the founders' understanding of property; there is no need to track the deviation to advance the book's thesis. While this chapter examines earlier decisions, I still stand by my earlier claim that the Constitution, and not precedent, should be what is binding. I provide a discussion of these earlier cases to provide a frame of reference for the nonspecialist and to show the specialist just where I depart from the standard reading of property rights.

Chapter 6 will provide a quantitative explanation of why certain states have acted to restrict *Kelo*-type seizures and others have decided to allow *Kelo*-type seizures. Drawing on the research of economists, political scientists, and legal scholars, I construct a model that shows the factors that affect a state's response to *Kelo*. Chapter 6 will show that property rights have become politicized, and the protection of those rights has become an ideologically and socially divisive issue. The result is that all rights become threatened, which then weakens the protection afforded to citizens by these rights. This chapter demonstrates the dramatic departure modern America has made from the origins outlined in chapters 1–4. In this chapter, I repeat some of the earlier discussion of the *Kelo* decision and the history of property rights in an effort to refresh the reader's mind and to allow the reader who may be interested in only the quantitative discussion to forgo the earlier chapters and read just the final two.

connect back to economics - class

If property rights cannot be shown to affect our daily lives, few people outside of academic circles will understand why they are important, or even care. In chapter 7, I look at the relationship between property rights and economic well-being. I begin by assimilating the work of economists who have uncovered the connection between property rights, legal structures, and economic well-being, and move on to my own analysis of the connection between property rights and economic well-being in the United States. By showing readers that the protection of property rights is positively correlated with economic prosperity, readers will see the practical implications of protecting private property.

As Leonard Levy argues, "If an economic right is involved, the Court never questions the reasonableness of the government's means. Economic rights, especially those of individuals, are inferior rights . . . economic due process of law, the old substantive due process, is dead even as to personal rights in property. The Court has abdicated the responsibility of judicial review in such cases, although it has not in any other Bill of Rights cases" (Levy 1995, p 14). This book provides historical and empirical support for this claim, discusses why it has occurred, and provides a normative critique of the development.

NOTES

1. I take this phrase from Albert W. Alschuler (2000).

2. My method could be termed *textualist,* but because my reading of the text is informed by those who originally penned the document, I consider there to be no functional difference between the two terms. I use *originalist* because when I go to the document, I try to understand it as those who wrote it understood it, thus trying to grasp its original meaning.

Chapter 1

Property Rights and the Common Law Tradition

To successfully promote economic development and secure individual liberties, the protection of private property must come first. The U.S. Constitution's protection of property rights can be traced to a number of sources. The colonial charters and state constitutions that came before the U.S. Constitution all had property rights provisions. But even those documents were not the genesis of property rights. To understand what property rights meant—in legal terms—for the drafters and ratifiers of the Constitution and the Bill of Rights, one must go to the source: the common law. The influence of the common law on the colonial generation is undeniable, and I will demonstrate how the common law's adherence to property rights found its way to America. In the course of doing so, I will go to the Magna Carta, Edward Coke, and William Blackstone—three of the most significant sources of common law thought. An examination of these sources will show that property rights deserve protection. This chapter will provide a historical and legal justification for a renewed interest in property rights. This point is best made by Bernard Siegan:

> For purposes of interpreting the United States Constitution, the most important meaning of a particular term is that given to it by its Framers and ratifiers. The evidence is persuasive that these people accepted the position of Blackstone and Coke that Chapter 39 (and Chapter 29 of a subsequent revision of the charter) had more than procedural meaning; it was meant to prevent the King from depriving his subjects of their rights . . . Blackstone stated that this chapter "alone would have merited the title that the Magna Carta bears, of the great charter." He construed the chapter as protecting "every individual of the nation in the free enjoyment of his life, his liberty, and his property, unless declared to be forfeited by the judgment of

1

his peers of the law of the land." Blackstone considered the rights of life, liberty, and property to be comprehended in the common law's "absolute rights of personal security, personal liberty, and private property." (Siegan 1997, p. 22)

This chapter will show that Siegan's claims regarding Blackstone are valid and that the same sentiment can be extended to the Magna Carta and Coke.

I begin with the Magna Carta simply because it is the clearest statement of the common law's position on the matters dealt with in this book. But, the reader should not be misled to think that the common law, and property rights, began with the Great Charter. Between 1164 and 1179, Henry II made great strides in protecting the rights of ownership. Beginning with the Constitutions of Clarendon, he showed his preference for jury trials in settling matters of disputed possession. This provision led to a weakening of the Church's claim of ownership of all land in England. Henry also oversaw provisions for the speedy remedy for a dispossessed freeholder, as such a freeholder was seen as not secure in his rights or possessions (Hogue 1986, p. 153). These provisions, and others that led up to the Magna Carta, show a strong attachment to property and a clear understanding that property must not be arbitrarily controlled by the government or Church.

While modern Americans may not be familiar with Coke, his influence on the revolutionary and founding generation is undeniable. His reading of the common law and justification for higher-law constitutionalism provided Americans with their sense of rights and limited government. Blackstone's influence was equally pervasive. Early Americans developed their understanding of common law and the Magna Carta via Coke and Blackstone. Due to Enlightenment influences, Americans developed their own strand of limited government, but the effects of common law can still be clearly seen.

This chapter will not give an itemized list of all things common law and their eventual adoption and development into the American system in the way I have done previously (Scott 2008). This chapter will deal with common law as a theory that was adopted by early Americans and adapted to their specific needs.

I. MAGNA CARTA

The Magna Carta is not a single document frozen in time. The Magna Carta was written and revised a number of times, and its history helps inform our understanding of the document. The first version of the document was signed in 1215 by John, King of England, and Ireland on the plains of Runnymede. Subsequent versions were introduced in 1225 and 1297. With each iteration, changes were made, and each change reinforced the principle that the law alone was sovereign. James Holt clearly expresses what I take to be the most accurate description of the progression of the Magna Carta by focusing on its natural law and ancient constitutional heritage:

> The Charter only survived alongside natural law by being raised to the same universal terms. Chapter 29 had become a convenient formulation of natural right. . . . The history of Magna Carta is the history not only of a document but also of an argument. . . . But the history of the argument is a history of a continuous element of political thinking. In this light there is no inherent reason why an assertion of law originally conceived in aristocratic interests should not be applied on a wider scale. If we can seek truth in Aristotle, we can seek it also in Magna Carta. The class and political interests involved in each stage of the Charter's history are one aspect of it; the principles it asserted, implied, or assumed are another. Approached as a political theory, it sought to establish the rights of subjects against authority and maintained the principle that authority was subject to law. If the matter is left in broad terms of sovereign authority on the one hand and the subject's rights on the other, this was the legal issue at stake in the fight against John, against Charles I, and in the resistance of the American colonists to George III. (Holt 1992, p. 8–9)

My concern is not with the document but with the argument. The argument expressed in the Magna Carta was taken up by Coke, Blackstone, and the American colonists. The argument is that of a political theory that recognizes the importance of the rule of law—thereby providing a due process of law—for the sole purpose of protecting one's life, liberty, and property. The right to life, liberty, and property has both intrinsic and instrumental values, whereas under the common law, due process has only an instrumental value, that of protecting life, liberty, and property. The instrumental and intrinsic value of the right to life, liberty, and property will receive its fullest expression through John Locke, who shows that property is the linchpin keeping all three together. But the common law provides the historical and legal basis for the rule of law. By examining the common law, we can come to understand the theory of self-rule as an instrumental value adopted by the American colonists.[1]

"It is universally agreed that the concept of 'due process of law' is rooted in Magna Carta, or the Great Charter, which was forced on John I by a group of feudal barons at Runnymede in 1215" (Gedicks 2008, p. 15). On June 19, 1215, in order to end the conflict between the barons and himself, King John signed the Magna Carta. Prior to signing, King John had taken arbitrary action against the barons through the Angevin judicial system, a group that was opposed to the feudal aristocracy. John had begun to infringe on the basic rights of the barons by making his word law, and his word generally went to the highest bidder:

> Too frequently, litigants came to the royal court and received no justice; law and judgment of the court were set aside for the will of John. Without reference to the law, John handed down arbitrary justice. Moreover, he denied the royal courts to numerous causes and parties, and he sold his justice at exorbitant prices to others. . . . The barons did not dislike the Angevin judicial system, but they came to fear it as a system upon which John could impose his capricious sense of justice; if John were to continue unrestricted, he would become a tyrant against whom there would be no protection of land and right. The barons, therefore, urgently felt that they must impose legal restrictions upon him. (Lyon 1980, p. 313)

At the heart of the Great Charter were due process protections that would prevent the King from imposing new rules and penalties without first adhering to a fair and proper process.[2] These rules were designed to protect the life, liberty, and property of all of the King's "archbishops, bishops, abbots, earls, barons, justices, foresters, sheriffs, stewards, servants, and to all his officials and loyal subjects." In chapter 52, King John agreed that anyone who "has been dispossessed or removed by us, without the legal judgment of his peers, from his lands, castles, or from his right, we will immediately restore them to him." Chapter 55 said that "fines, made with us unjustly and against the law of the land, shall be entirely remitted." Chapters 20–22 provided equivalent protection for merchants, freemen, clergy, and barons. Chapter 39 was the boldest statement of due process. The chapter reads:

> No freeman shall be taken, or imprisoned, or disseized, or outlawed, or exiled, or in any way harmed—nor will we go upon or send upon him—save by the lawful judgment of his peers or by the law of the land. (Magna Carta, 1215)

This chapter protected all freemen from improper deprivation of their lives, liberties, or properties without due process. Noted historian Charles McIlwain wrote of chapter 39 that it "was merely the classical statement of a fundamental principle that the King may not take the definition of rights into his own hands, but must proceed against none by force for any alleged violation of them until a case has been made out against such a one by 'due process of law'" (McIlwain 1947, p. 86). In writing about the English Constitution, philosopher David Hume argued, "Men acquired some more security for their properties and their liberties: And government approached a little nearer to that end, for which it was originally instituted. . . . And thus, the establishment of the Great Charter . . . became a kind of epoch in the constitution" (Hume 1975, p. 236).

Chapter 39 of the 1215 Charter shows the centrality of life, liberty, and property. Depending on who is consulted, there are at least twelve property provisions in the original charter. This has led historians such as Arthur Hogue to conclude that

> the common law of the twelfth and thirteenth centuries is in large part the law of the law of land and tenures, the law of property rights and services together with rules of procedure for the administration of justice. A glance at the chapters of Magna Carta or at any collection of common-law writs will reveal the dominant concern with rights in land: the possessor, or seisin, of land, the services owed for the tenure of land, the inheritance of land, the leasing of land, the wardship of land, the profits from land, the burdens of land, and the wrongs of land. (Hogue 1986, p. 107)

The confusion over how many provisions deal directly and exclusively with property is caused by the interrelated characteristic of rights as understood by the Magna Carta. Rights that restricted government action—due process rights—were instituted for the protection of life, liberty, and property. But life, liberty, and property were not always distinguishable from one another or from due process rights. For instance, in chapter 4 it is stated:

> The guardian of the land of an heir who is under age shall take from it only reasonable revenues, customary dues, and feudal services. He shall do this without destruction or damage to men or property. If we have given the guardianship of the land to a sheriff, or to any person answerable to us for the revenues, and he commits destruction or damage, we will exact compensation from him, and the land shall be entrusted to two worthy and prudent men of the same 'fee,' who shall be answerable to us for the revenues, or to the person to whom we have assigned them. . . . (Magna Carta, 1215)

A similar provision is provided in chapter 5 which states more precisely how the law protects a land owner against unjust acts against the land from the land's guardian. What can be inferred from chapter 4, and is explicitly stated in other parts of the Charter—specifically chapters 28, 30, 31, and 39—is that to unduly strip someone of his property is to strip him of other rights as well.

It is recognized by nearly all sensible people that a government must be able to generate revenue in order to survive, but how it does so should be limited so that the threat of tyranny is restrained as no government can be legitimate that takes from its people in a manner inconsistent with private good for a purpose which is inconsistent with the public good. Chapter 9 of the 1215 Charter recognizes this point where it states, "Neither we nor our officials will seize any land or rent in payment of a debt, so long as the debtor has movable goods sufficient to discharge the debt. A debtor's sureties shall not be distrained upon so long as the debtor himself can discharge his debt" (Magna Carta, 1215).

While chapter 39 justifiably receives the most attention—partly because of its reputation with entrepreneur Lord Coke—it is chapters 28, 30, and 31 that provide explicit protections against property seizures:

> No constable or other bailiff of ours shall take the corn or other chattels of any one except he straightway give money for them, or can be allowed a respite in that regard by the will of the seller. (Magna Carta, 1215, chapter 28)
> No sheriff nor bailiff of ours, nor any one else, shall take the horses or carts of any freeman for transport, unless by the will of that freeman. (Magna Carta, 1215, chapter 30)
> Neither we nor our bailiffs shall take another's wood for castles or for other private uses, unless by the will of him to whom the wood belongs. (Magna Carta, 1215, chapter 31)

These provisions prohibit a taking of physical property unless the owner has consented to it or is justly compensated. If the taking is for an explicit private use, the owner of the property must offer his consent, as compensation does not justify a private taking. It is only when there is an explicit public purpose that compensation is adequate. The manner in which property is treated is consistent with the manner in which life and liberty are treated in the other chapters of the Great Charter. In order to take someone's life, liberty, or property, the government must do so in a way that respects the rights of the individual. Government cannot act haphazardly; it too must be subject to the law.

The original charter was short-lived however. On August 24, 1215, the Charter was repealed. But, even the repeal did not last long as King Henry reinstated it a short while after he took over the throne in October 1216 following the death of King John. King Henry was only a child when he inherited the Crown at the age of nine. To win favor with the barons in order to protect what might have been perceived as a weak king, Henry's advisors revised and reinstated the Magna Carta. When the charter was reissued in 1225, it contained only thirty-eight chapters but was proclaimed to be a reissue of the original Charter. The commitment to the original Charter was clear, as seen in chapter 29 of the new charter which expanded and clarified chapter 39 of the original. In the new Charter chapter 29 reads:

> No freeman shall be taken, or imprisoned, or be disseised of his freehold, or liberties, or free customs, or be outlawed, or exiled, or any otherwise destroyed;

nor will we not pass upon him, nor condemn him, but by lawful judgment of his peers, or by the law of the land. We will sell to no man, we will not deny or defer to any man either justice or right. (Magna Carta, 1225)

Revisions were made in other places as well, but all within the spirit of the earlier 1215 Charter and all pushing forward the idea that the law was sovereign. Chapters 19 and 21 of the new Charter made the same provisions as chapters 28, 30, and 31 in the 1215 version. Consistent with chapters 19, 21, and 29 in the 1225 Charter, Parliament adopted provisions to augment these chapters. The intention was to provide protection against arbitrary property seizures and deprivations, much like the Fifth Amendment in the U.S. Constitution. In 1331, King Edward III oversaw the adoption of a provision which read, "That no Man from henceforth shall be attached by any Accusation, nor forjudged of Life or Limb, nor his Lands, Tenements, Goods, nor Chattels seized into the King's Hands, against the form of the Great Charter and the Law of the Land." Twenty-one years later, a similar provision was adopted, still under Edward III, "That from henceforth none shall be taken . . . unless it be by Indictment or Presentment of good and lawful People of the same neighborhood where such Deeds be done, in due Manner, or be Process made by Writ original at the Common Law; not that none be out of his Franchises, nor his Freeholds, unless he be due brought into answer . . . by the course of law. . . ." Two years later, another provision was added that echoed the earlier language, stating, in effect, that in order for one's body or land to be taken into custody, it must be done according to "due Process of the Law."

The Magna Carta reflects the common law's commitment to the due process of law, the supremacy of law, and the idea that the preservation of life, liberty, and property is the proper end of government. The Magna Carta protects citizens against illegitimate government action and defines all government action inconsistent with the rule of law as illegitimate. This places the man and ruler on equal footing, thus granting greater protection to man's rights. In doing so it laid the groundwork for a justification for the American Revolution and provided a historical and legal precedent for those provisions relating to property and due process found in the Constitution and Bill of Rights.

The "Ancient Constitution"—captured by the Magna Carta—has its roots in tradition and natural law. The traditions were reflections of natural law; therefore, the traditions embodied in the ancient constitution were natural law, and thus no man could be above the rule of law. By grounding its authority in tradition, the ancient constitution was perceived to be grounded in notions of habituation, wisdom, and consent (Goldberg 2005, p. 9), thus granting it more authority than positive law. The ancient constitution provided stability in the governing structure and provided legal remedies for wrongful deprivations of life, liberty, and property (Goldberg 2005, p. 8). Found in the ancient constitution was the protection of property that ensured prosperity (Sommerville 1999, p. 20). But more than an instrumental right, the right to property was understood to have an intrinsic value.

The Magna Carta, like all common law, is grounded in a tradition whose origins are beyond memory. "The coincidence of widespread belief in the ancient roots of the Charter's rights and remedies with purported discovery by royal courts of a similarly ancient common law, indelibly linked the Charter and the common law in the English legal tradition" (Gedicks 2008, p. 17). To bring it to life and give it force, common law, and thus the Magna Carta, needed advocates. The precise meaning of the Magna Carta would be determined by common law judges, the most famous of which was Edward Coke.

> According to the great justice Sir Edward Coke and others, Magna Carta had saved England from the rule of tyrants, had consecrated basic civil and political rights, and had germinated English constitutional government. More specifically, they declared that it put the King under law, limited his actions by the collective will of the nation, provided that there would be no taxation without parliamentary consent and guaranteed in ringing terms that all men of England should have due process of the law and trial by jury. (Lyons 1980, p. 310–311)

There is some contention over whether the Magna Carta deserves such high praise, but the fact remains that it is the source we go to when looking for the rights of Englishmen, and there is no better expositor of this tradition than Coke.[3]

II. COKE

Lord Coke dedicated a large portion of his *Second Institute* of his *Institutes of the Laws of England* to the Magna Carta of 1225. Coke writes, "by due process of the common law, no man shall be put to answer without presentment before justices, or thing of record, or by due process, or by writ original" (Coke 1979, 50). Consequently, he viewed the common law as a restraint on the powers of the monarchy and other governmental bodies. Coke understood due process to be found at common law when he writes that no man should be deprived of liberty or possessions, "without being brought in to answer but by due process of the common law" (Coke 1974, p. 50). Coke goes on to write that, "the law of the land might extend to all, it is said *per legem terra* [by the law of the land]" (Coke 1974, p. 50). "It was also in the *Institutes* that Coke clearly equated the 'law of the land' with the 'due process of law'" (Gedicks 2008, p. 30). Both phrases were adopted by American constitutionalists prior to and after 1789, but it was due process of law that was incorporated into the Bill of Rights. However, the common law's reliance on the phrase "law of the land" gives credence to Arthur Hogue's claim that the common law was the law of land and tenures. But in the common law, as elaborated by Coke, land had a dual meaning: first as physical land and second as a security for life and liberty. While the dual meaning of property will not be fully developed until Locke does so in his *Second Treatise* (§87), it is important to understand that property had both an intrinsic and instrumental value—or rather, it could be conceived as a substantive and procedural right—because it was this dual meaning of property that was incorporated into the American constitutional tradition by James Madison.

While having fallen into disuse in the fourteenth through sixteenth centuries, Coke revived the Magna Carta, and with it, higher-law constitutionalism, from which he reconstituted the fundamental limits on Crown prerogatives. The limits were not on the Crown alone: Coke placed Parliament under the rule of law as well. As presented by Frederick Gedicks (2008, p. 19–20), Coke's argument for placing King and Parliament under law followed a simple syllogism: (1) the Magna Carta declared the existence of fundamental English laws and customs that formed part of the common law; (2) by ruling the kingdom in violation of these laws and customs, King John had been a tyrant; (3) therefore, any ruler who failed to observe the Magna Carta likewise violated the common law and was similarly guilty of tyrannous behavior. "By treating Magna Carta and the liberties it declared as 'constitutional' law possessed of a more fundamental status than ordinary law, Coke meant to invest Magna Carta with a place in the English system that was prior to and more foundational than the actions of crown or, perhaps, even parliament" (Gedicks 2008, p. 20).

As discussed in the previous section, chapter 29 of the Great Charter provided many of those rights that are captured in the American Bill of Rights. What is important to note, is that as understood by Coke, there was virtually no distinction between procedural (instrumental) and substantive (intrinsic) rights. Procedural rights had the instrumental value of ensuring other rights. Without procedural rights, one cannot have a fair trial, and it is only through a fair trial—thus having the protections of the law—that one can hope to achieve justice. In a more general sense, the rule of law is upheld through procedures designed for that purpose. But there is an intrinsic value to procedural rights. Because these rights ensure freedom, they are markers of freedom. Without the proper procedures, the rights of individuals become threatened; therefore, procedural rights become substantive rights by the fact that they are inextricably linked with the rights they ensure.[4] "He [Coke] again maintained that

Chapter 29 and Magna Carta generally were declarations of the ancient rights of Englishmen, and thus limits on the actions of both crown and parliament. . . . The liberty protected by Chapter 29, according to Coke, 'signifieth the freedoms, that the Subjects of England have,' meaning substantive as well as procedural rights" (Gedicks 2008, p. 31).[5] Thus under the common law, there was a unity of rights. There was no preference given to one set of rights over another, as Coke understood that substantive (intrinsic) rights cannot stand without procedural (instrumental) rights, and procedural rights have no purpose other than providing substantive benefits. Look at it from a different angle. To sacrifice intrinsic rights for instrumental rights would lead one into tyranny. Conversely, to sacrifice instrumental rights for intrinsic rights would lead one into anarchy. Of course there were certain rights, such as property, which had intrinsic and instrumental value, which then made them both substantive and procedural due process rights.

While the Magna Carta provided a paper barrier against unjust government action, it established no authority that could keep Crown or Parliament within the bounds of the law. Coke reasoned that it ought to be the role of English judges to interpret the common law and to keep the law as sovereign, with every branch subservient to it. "The judges had applied the common law to limit the king's powers as well as those of localities and guilds" (Siegan 2001, p. 15). Coke told the Parliament in 1628 that, "Magna Carta is such a fellow that he will have no Sovereign" (Gough 1971, p. 64). Although the common law, and thus the Magna Carta, was sovereign over judges, judges had a unique role in the interpretation of the law given their vantage point and training. Coke's vision of the law was adapted in the American scheme which sought to establish a nation of laws and not of men. Also, Coke's vision of the judiciary was adopted by the American founders as well (Stoner 1992; Scott 2008).[6]

Coke's position on the role of the judiciary is most famously displayed in *Dr. Bonham's Case*. Thomas Bonham brought action for wrongful imprisonment against the president and censors of the College of Physicians in London. Bonham had been practicing medicine without a license, and the College of Physicians put him in jail. Coke presided over the case as the Chief Justice of the Court of Common Pleas. Coke reasoned that the College of Physicians acted against the common law as it sat in judgment on a case in which it was a party. Also, because the power of the College of Physicians as the sole body with the authority to license someone to practice medicine was given to it by Parliament, this became a case of a parliamentary act coming into conflict with the common law. The decision of the Court was to decide for the plaintiff on the grounds that the statute violated common law principles in that the right to imprison granted to the college was not for the benefit of the public but for the maintenance of a monopoly. In the case, Coke wrote:

And it appears in our books, that in many cases, the common law will control acts of parliament, and sometimes adjudge them to be utterly void: for when an act of parliament is against common right and reason, or repugnant, or impossible to be performed, the common law will control it, and adjudge such act to be void.

There is considerable disagreement over just what this phrase means (Stoner 1992) and whether it grants the Court the authority to strike down any and all laws that are found contrary to common law. In discussing *Dr. Bonham's Case,* and thus the rule of law, Gedicks quotes Orth who writes:

Coke had been defending not only Dr. Bonham's right to a fair trial but also the law's supremacy over the powers that be. Coke was trying to give content to the law's restraint on power; that is, he was trying to give substance to due process. There were, he thought, things that the supreme power in the state, even the king in Parliament, could not lawfully do, no matter how hard he tried. (Gedicks 2008, p. 26)

But, it is my understanding that the case demonstrates the commitment on behalf of Coke to common law principles in the face of a parliamentary act to the contrary, while granting no credence to the claim that judges are superior to Parliament. Let us not forget that statutes are part of the common law, but some statutes can act against the public benefit, and the Court must balance the two competing interests. But, this granted judges the authority—though rarely practiced—to decide on common law grounds even in cases where the Parliament had already spoken. Siegan states a similar position when he writes:

Coke offered a much less drastic remedy for the tyranny of the legislature [than Locke]. He asserted that the courts are empowered to apply the common law and annul legislation contrary to it. Notwithstanding the great authority of a legislature under a parliamentary system, Coke believed in the power of the judiciary to protect an owner from governmental abridgement of his property and other fundamental rights. (Siegan 1997, p. 17)

In another instance of judicial review, Coke came into direct conflict with the King's order. In reaction to Coke's writs of prohibition against ecclesiastical courts from taking equity claims, the Archbishop of Canterbury appealed to the King's authority. Coke denied the Archbishop's claim and in his decision said that judges had the necessary reason to make such decisions. King James replied that he and others had reason and reason was not a trait of common law judges alone; therefore, the writ of prohibitions should be repealed. In reply to James, Coke wrote in *Prohibitions del Roy:*

His majesty was not learned in the laws of his realm of England, and causes which concern the life, or goods, or fortunes of his subjects, are not to be decided by natural reason, but by the artificial reason and judgment of law, which law is an act which requires long study and experience, before that a man can attain to the cognizance of it. (Coke 2004, Vol. I, p. 481)

Needless to say, James was not pleased, but at this time Coke escaped reprimand. Perhaps this is why Coke did not stop making comments to this effect, nor was he the only common law jurist to make such statements. Another common law jurist said that, "The common law is a reasonable usage throughout the whole realm approved time out of mind in the King's court of record which have jurisdiction over the whole kingdom, to be good and profitable for the commonwealth" (Hedley quoted by Postema 2002, p. 166).

Therefore, one of the reasons judges hold the unique position of being the interpreters of the common law is because they possess the necessary training and knowledge, which reflects the artificial reason found in common law. Coke gives support to this argument by saying, "The Law is like a deep well, and he that reacheth deepest sees the amiable and admirable secrets of the Law, wherein the Sages of the Law in ancient Times have had the deepest Reach" (Coke 1979, p. 71). In this statement, one can see the inductive process that animates common law reasoning. Understanding the common law, and Coke's take on it in particular, requires that one understand the thought process of a common law jurist in order to understand how the common law differs from positive law. The reason of jurists, and the reason of the common law, is artificial reason. That it is artificial does not make it a false kind of reason, but a reason that is unique to common law jurists and the common law. "The law, to Coke, is thus a science in something like the Aristotelian sense of practical science, joining reason and knowledge of particulars, yet contained not in books as a body of knowledge but in the minds of those who can use it" (Stoner 1992, p. 18).[7] To this, Stoner adds, "the most significant principle in Coke's understanding of the law is his insistence upon the equation of law and reason . . ." (Stoner 1992, p. 22). This is a common point found in Stoner, perhaps the most authoritative political theorist on matters of common law, who in another instance writes:

The common law proceeds by reason, but by reason that collects and judges particulars—by a sort of Aristotelian practical reason—rather than by reason in the modern, Enlightenment, analytical sense—the reason that breaks apart and reassembles. It stresses continuity rather than novelty, though it demands some reason greater than custom alone, for by common law, unreasonable customs have no legal force. (Stoner 1992, p. 177)

Because of the process by which judges make their decisions, and the training and experience which they draw upon in making their decisions, the common law is reason. But it is a reason that respects the changing demands and needs of the society in which it serves. Precedents are guideposts that show what has been done before, but they are not binding on a judge because facts change, and each case deserves its own unique treatment. But, as more opinions are made, and the experience and training of judges culminates in successive opinions, the knowledge of the law improves as it begins to reflect the reason of men who respect law and tradition. On this point, Coke writes in Part I of the *Institutes:*

For reason is the life of the Law, nay the Common Law itself is nothing else but reason, which is to be understood of an artificial perfection of reason gotten by long study, observation and experience and not every man's natural reason. . . . This legal reason is the highest reason. . . . And therefore if all the reason that is dispersed into so many several heads were united into one, yet could he not make such a Law as the Law of England is, because by many succession of ages it hath been fined and refined by an infinite number of grave and learned men, and by long experience grown to such a perfection for the government of this real, as the old rule may be justly verified of it. . . . No man (out of his own private reason) ought to be wiser than the Law, which is the perfection of reason. (Coke 1999, p. 495)

Of course, had Coke made this statement in only one instance it would be less convincing, but he repeated the position many times:

We are but of yesterday (and therefore had need of the wisdom of those that were before us) and had been ignorant (if we had not received light and knowledge from our forefathers) and our days upon the earth are but as a shadow, in respect of the old ancient days and times past, wherein the laws have been by the wisdom of the most excellent men, in many successions of ages, by long and continual experience (the trial of light and truth) fined and refined, which no man (being short of time) albeit he had in his head the wisdom of all the men in the world, in any one age could ever have effected or attained unto. (*Calvin's Case*, 7th Coke Report 4a, 77 ER 381)

Artificial reason is manufactured by men, but not from first principles, from experience with human affairs. The artificial reason of the common law does not lend itself to a definitive formulation either. The common law, with its artificial reason, is a fusion of reason and experience in which neither is the final authority. "Reason is not original and comprehensive; rather, it takes what is given and works upon it, improves it. It does this by bringing to bear no logic alone, but logic together with wide learning. The reason Coke appeals to is not a theoretical but a practical faculty. It is certainly not mere discretion, but neither is it logic devoid of experience. It is a trained way of thinking, not arbitrary but also no apodictic" (Stoner 1992, p. 23).

Even though it seemingly defies simple categorization, scholars have not stopped trying. The six components of artificial reason, as seen by Gerald Postema (2003), are: (1) it is *pragmatic,* as it focuses on practical problem-solving; (2) it has a *public mission,* which means it seeks to solve problems with the public in mind; (3) artificial reason is *contextual,* which means judges have knowledge of experience and study, not abstract principles; (4) because it is practical and not theoretic, artificial reason is *nonsystematic.* "On this view, the law is to be found in the accumulated experience recorded in the books and memories of common law jurists, not in any theory, or articulation of this experience. Law is practice, not a theoretical representation of it" (Postema 2003, p. 6); (5) Artificial reason is *discursive,* meaning, arguments are made about the law prior to the facts being introduced which lead to a deliberative reasoning and argument about the law; (6) artificial reason, like the common law in general, is *common,* which means "it was the practice of public forensic argument, situated and moving about in a world of recorded experience of 'human affairs and conversation'" (Postema 2003, p. 9). Therefore, for Postema—who puts forth a position similar to Stoner's—Coke's artificial reason is called artificial not because "it rests on some special insight or intuition vouchsafed only to those initiated into the professional mysteries, but rather because it is the disciplined practice of argument and disputation in a public forum. . . . It is 'artificial' in the sense of being the product of reflective practical experience, as opposed to untutored individual intuition or a natural capacity for deductive reasoning exercised in abstraction from the concrete details of ordinary life" (Postema 2003, p. 10).

One can see then why it is judges and not the Parliament or Crown who have the power to interpret law and why the law is sovereign, even over judges. But to understand the common law, particularly as it relates to rights, one must look at decisions made at common law. Because this book focuses on eminent domain, I will use three takings cases decided by Coke to illustrate this point.

While sitting as Chief Justice on the Court of Common Pleas, Coke decided the *Case of the King's Prerogative in Saltpeter* (1606).[8] A landowner appealed the act of the King's men who seized saltpeter from his land. The King made the argument that the saltpeter was to be used in making ammunition for the national defense, and thus for the common good. Coke and his Court decided in favor of the King but placed some restrictions on his prerogative. First, the King must use it for the national defense and not for his own purpose. Second, no other property of the landowner's may be damaged in digging up the saltpeter. Third, the landowner can take his own saltpeter from the land, which would make the saltpeter not accessible to the King under this prerogative. It is only when the saltpeter lay in the land that it is made available to the King.

In 1610, Coke heard a case in which the King's commissioners ordered fifteen towns on the Isle of Ely to build a new river and repair the existing drainage systems. In addition to paying for the work, the people of Ely objected to the taking of their land in order to make the necessary changes. In the *Case of the Isle of Ely,* Coke decided that the King could not give the power of eminent domain to the commissioners nor could the taxes be imposed on those who would not benefit from the new drainage system. Coke based his argument on the fact that the drainage system improvements were not absolutely necessary and that such a prerogative was only appropriate for the Parliament.[9]

Both of these cases are consistent with the precedent Coke established in *Mouse's Case* (1600), in which property seizure was justified so long as it was required for the preservation of liberty and property. While on rough seas, one of the passengers on a commercial barge threw overboard one of the other passenger's belongings in order to help lighten the load and keep the boat from sinking. The Court upheld this action, reasoning that without destroying that person's property all life and property would have been lost. This poses a problem in that one person suffered a disproportionate share of the responsibility, but because the conflict was between two private citizens, there was no recourse, though the Court left the possibility open that had it been done by an agent of the government, there would have been a remedy available.

As stated at the outset of this chapter and repeated at the outset of this section, the common law was the law of land. At the center of the rights codified in the Magna Carta was property. Therefore, to understand the role and importance of property, one must have first read some of Coke's takings cases. But to understand the importance on the limits of takings, one must understand the importance of property. And while Coke does not provide the type of defense of property rights that is found in Locke or Madison, he does provide an adequate legal defense. In interpreting chapter 29 of the Magna Carta, Coke writes of nine separate branches. According to Bernard Siegan,

> The second branch (prohibiting disseising) . . . Coke construed broadly to include considerable protection of ownership: "No man shall be disseised, that is, put out of seisin, or dispossessed of his free-hold (that is) lands, or livelihood, or of his liberties, or free-customes, that is of such franchise, and freedoms, and free-customes, as belong to him by his free birth right, unless it be by the lawful judgment, that is, verdict of his equals (that is, of men of his own condition) or by the law of the land (that is, to speak it once for all) by the due course, and process of law." (Siegan 2001, p. 13–14)

Coke states elsewhere, according to Siegan, that no land or property can be seized contrary to the law of the land. And as stated earlier in this section, Coke defines law of the land as due process of law, and due process of law is found in the common law, most specifically in the Magna Carta. The due process provisions that stipulate the procedures that must be adhered to in order to classify a takings as legitimate are the most important for Coke.

Bernard Siegan is not the only one to see the importance of property in Coke's writing and decisions. Stoner writes that for Coke, "Property rights are not simply useful conventions for dividing up social wealth; the many rights in and about what we call property are for Coke ancient and vested privileges, and it is of the utmost importance to him that they be justly settled" (Stoner 1992, p. 19). To repeat a point raised earlier, and that will be raised throughout the book, there is a unity of rights that is captured in common law thinking that has been sacrificed in modern American politics. For property rights serve as both intrinsic and instrumental rights. And for those rights that can be categorized as purely instrumental or purely intrinsic, it is important to remember that each relies on the other for existence and value.

Despite modern America's deviation from its common law origin (Scott 2008), Coke was held in high regard among American colonists. The colonists brought with them the common law of England and made required reading out of Coke for most colonial lawyers. According to Edward Corwin, in the colonies, Coke "was first on the ground" (Corwin 1928, p. 394). Coke was the embodiment of the common law. His authority was so strong that later commentators have written, "that it is useless to contend that 'he was either misled by his sources or unconsciously misinterpreted them,' for Coke's mistakes, it is said, are the common law" (Brockelbank 1954, p. 562). Bernard Siegan writes, "English and American courts accepted and cited Coke's interpretation of Chapter 29 as authoritative on the meaning of the 'law of the land' and the 'due process of law,' and numerous U.S. federal and state judicial opinions have cited him in various matters" (Siegan 2001, p. 12–13).

American jurists after the colonial period continued to show marks of his influence, particularly on matters of judicial review. According to Chancellor James Kent:

[I]n republics it [the judiciary] is equally salutary, in protecting the constitution and laws from encroachment. . . . It is requisite that the courts of justice should be able, at all times, to present a determined countenance against all licentious acts; and to give them the firmness to do it. . . . (Kent 1836, p. 294)

But it was Coke's arguments for rights, more than his position on the judiciary, that had the most noticeable impact. The common law protections articulated by Coke and found in the Magna Carta were brought to America. On September 5, 1774, the First Continental Congress declared that the rights of inhabitants of America are secured "by the immutable laws of nature, the principles of the English Constitution, and the several charters or compacts pursuant to which the colonial governments were established . . . the respective colonies are entitled to the common law of England" (Tansill 1972, p. 1–2). By the time the Bill of Rights was ratified, all thirteen of the former colonies put provisions into their state constitutions that were influenced by chapter 29 of the Great Charter, 1225. Even the Northwest Ordinance provided a commitment to due process by saying, "no man shall be deprived of his life, liberty, or property, but by the judgment of his peers or the law of the land" (Tansill 1972, p. 48). Of course, the precise import of the common law on the American founding is the topic of chapters 3 and 4 of this book.

But when succinctly summarized, as Siegan (2001) did, one is immediately struck by the similarities between Coke's common law and the American constitutional tradition. As a jurist and legal scholar, Coke put forth the ideas that no man can be deprived of life, liberty, or property except under due process of law (2 Coke, *Institutes* 46–47, 50–51); the King and Parliament are subject to the laws, thereby protecting citizens from illegitimate deprivation of life, liberty, or property; judges must uphold the principles of due process of law, even over parliamentary acts (2 Coke, *Institutes* 45–46, 51 and *Dr. Bonham's Case*), property rights can only be limited when the limitation is necessary for the preservation of life and property (*Mouse's Case*); and regulations, repairs, and seizures can only be done when they benefit the public and the burden is equitably distributed (2 Coke, *Institutes* 41 and *Isle of Ely*).

While there are profound differences between Coke and William Blackstone on the role of the judiciary, there are equally profound similarities in their positions on the role of government, rule of law, and property rights.[10] Blackstone wrote in reference to the common law that no person's land or goods can be or should be seized without recourse to the law of the land, which required also his consent (1. Chapter 1).

III. BLACKSTONE

If what Michael Zuckert says is true—that the American tradition is an amalgamation of common law and Enlightenment principles reflected in Blackstone's thought—then moving past Blackstone in a study of property rights in the American context would be misguided, given that the American

conception of property rights is an amalgamation of philosophical and legal
principles found in the Enlightenment and common law. To better understand
this point, I will work through Blackstone to show the amalgamation that has
informed American jurisprudence and theory of property rights. This will
serve as a prelude to chapters 2–4.

While Blackstone follows in the tradition of Coke, he departs in several
significant ways that will be outlined here. Despite their differences, both
scholars find liberty in the common law. Blackstone, more than Coke, seeks
to bring a higher level of certainty to the common law through the application
of scientific reasoning. The introductory sections of the *Commentaries* state
in numerous instances that the intention of the work is to bring an enlightened
science to the unsystematic state of the common law (1. Section 9, and 1,
Introduction, Section 1).[11] Instead of an inductive system supported by Coke,
Blackstone implemented first principles in order to make the common law a
deductive system so that arguments can be "drawn *a priori,* from the spirit of
the laws and the natural foundations of justice" (1, Introduction, Section 1).
For Coke, the law is bound by ancient customs and the consciousness of the
community, waiting to be discovered, not made, by judges. While Blackstone
recognized the importance of custom and community consciousness, he
moved closer to a theory of positivism and away from Coke's artificial reasoning. "Blackstone, like Coke, defends the common law, but he does so in
a way that shows he has absorbed Hobbes's critique . . . obviously under the
spell of a modern scientific view of nature. . . . For Blackstone, as we have
seen, that first principle is self-love; for the earlier thinkers, it was synderesis,
the faculty of soul that contained the first precepts of actions: seek the good
and flee the evil" (Zuckert 2002, p. 243, 246, 251).

To understand Blackstone's jurisprudence and theory of property rights,
one must come to appreciate his unique amalgamation of common law rights
and natural rights.

His [Blackstone's] claim on our attention derives . . . from his contribution to
the "truly remarkable occurrence that stands at the opening of the [American]
tradition: the assimilation by the natural rights philosophy of a variety of
what are often thought to be competing traditions of political thought." "The
American political tradition . . . consists precisely in the unique amalgam so
constructed." . . . They [Americans] spoke equally strenuously of their rights as
rights of Englishmen . . . but they also spoke of their rights as natural rights. . . .
It was one of the more significant dimensions of the American amalgam that it
brought together these two types of rights. . . . Efforts to amalgamate natural
rights and common law surely predate Blackstone . . . but nobody worked out
the synthesis so thoroughly. . . . The 'rights of Englishmen,' secured by the
common law and the constitution, turn out to be "no other, than the residuum of

natural liberty, which is not required by the laws of society to be sacrificed to public convenience; or else those civil privileges, which society hath engaged to provide, in lieu of the natural liberties so given up by individuals." . . . the rights of Englishmen "were formerly . . . the rights of all mankind; but in most other countries of the world being now more or less debased and destroyed, they may be said to remain, in a peculiar and emphatical manner, the rights of the people of England." (Zuckert 2003, p. 41–42)

For Blackstone, natural law is created by God, but requires man to make it real in the sense that a law that is not enforced or known does not serve the purpose of law, which is to restrain and direct behavior that upsets civil society. Assumed by this understanding of natural law is the implication that natural law cannot enforce itself, but requires human law that is in accord with reason, and thus natural law, to enforce it. This departs only slightly from Coke's understanding of artificial reason in which Coke draws on the medieval understanding of natural law, which is law granted by God, but only manifests itself through the continual examination of community conflicts by judges. As Blackstone writes:

As God, when he created matter, endued it with a principle of mobility, established certain rules for the perpetual direction of that motion; so, when he created man, and endued him with freewill to conduct himself in all parts of life, he laid down certain immutable laws of nature, whereby that freewill is to some degree regulation and restrained, and gave him also the faculty of reason to discover the purport of those laws. (1, Introduction, Section 2)

Unfortunately, Blackstone is confined by the nature of the natural law discussion, and therefore, any attempt to define the law ends up being a bit vague. Perhaps this is the reason he looked to human law, as an extension of natural law, for authority over human actions. For instance, as Alschuler writes, "According to Blackstone, the test of whether an action comported with natural law was whether it 'tends to man's real happiness . . . or, on the other hand . . . is destructive of man's real happiness.' . . . Blackstone saw justice both as an end in itself and as a means to an end—the attainment of human happiness. The law of nature accorded with both external and internal criteria of value" (Alschuler 1996, p. 23). While such an understanding of law is helpful by defining for us the ends of the law, it does not do much for matters of practice. That is, if each man can define for himself his own happiness, conflict will inevitably result. Thus, human law is required to restrict men's actions and to settle disputes when man acts beyond the restrictions of human law. So while he looked to natural law for guidance, he attributed to human law an equal—if not higher—station. Blackstone finds in the common law a proper balance between manmade law and natural law. Similar to Coke's artificial reasoning, common law carries the practical characteristics of human law and the force of natural law because at common law "the goodness of a custom depends on its having been used time out of mind; or, in the solemnity of our legal phrase, time whereof memory of man runneth not to the contrary" (1, Introduction, Section 3).

As a result of Blackstone's ambition to bring about a systematic understanding of the law based on first principles, he inevitably created a legal positivism that brings him toward Hobbes and away from the common law tradition of Coke. According to Blackstone, the common law "is positive law, fixed and established by custom, which custom is evidenced by judicial decisions" (1, Introduction, Section 3). When he raises the question of who has authority over the common law, he says:

> The answer is, by the judges of the several courts of justice. They are the depositary of the laws; the living oracles, who must decide in all cases of doubt, and who are bound by an oath to decide according to the law of the land. . . . And indeed these judicial decisions are the principle and most authoritative evidence, that can be given, of the existence of such a custom as shall form a part of the common law. (1, Introduction, Section 3)

In the same section of the *Commentaries,* he gives a greater force to precedent than does Coke:

> For it is an established rule to abide by former precedents, where the same points come again in litigation; as well to keep the scale of justice even and steady, and not liable to waver with every new judge's opinion; as also because the law in that case being solemnly declared and determined, what before was uncertain, and perhaps indifferent, is now become a permanent rule, which it is not in the breast of any subsequent judge to alter or vary from . . . he being sworn to determine . . . according to the known laws and customs of the land. . . . (1, Introduction, Section 3)

The argument from a recent book on American common law suggests that "Blackstone departs from other common law scholars when he tries to explain the development of the law through reason" with the aim of achieving a rational explanation of the law. For, "once this rational explanation has been achieved, and first principles extracted, the law can be applied universally, according to Blackstone, in order to promote liberty and justice through the law" (Scott 2008, p. 128). Blackstone's common law carries traits of rational scientific inquiry that create a positivist conception of the law and take what was inductive and makes it deductive. The following quote shows just how far removed Blackstone is from Coke's position on the law:

[R]eason with precision, and separate argument from fallacy, by the clear simple rules of pure unsophisticated logic; if he can fix his attention, and steadily pursue truth through any the most intricate deduction, by the use of mathematical demonstrations; if he has enlarged his conceptions . . . by a view of the several branches of genuine, experimental, philosophy; if he has impressed on his mind the sound maxims of the law of nature, the best and most authentic foundation of human laws; if, lastly, he has contemplated those maxims reduced to a practical system in the laws of imperial Rome . . . a student thus qualified may enter upon the study of law. . . . (1, Introduction, Section 1)

Jurists are given a great deal of autonomy. The autonomy of judges is required because of his formulation of the relationship between natural law and human law. While human law is superior to natural law in the sense that it provides a restraint on men's actions, human laws must conform to natural law, as it is understood through reason. Blackstone writes:

Yet this rule admits of exception, where the former determination is most evidently contrary to reason; much more if it be contrary to divine law. But even in such cases the subsequent judges do not pretend to make a new law, but to vindicate the old one from misrepresentation. For if it be found . . . manifestly absurd or unjust it is declared, not that such a sentence is bad law, but that it is not law . . . the law is the perfection of reason, that it always intends to conform thereto, and that what is not reason is not law. (1, Introduction, Section 3)

So in the course of justifying judicial review, Blackstone returns to Coke's understanding of common law when he admits that judges do not make law, they merely discover what has always been, and if some new law comes into conflict with reason, judges may overturn it. Therefore, if we are to stick with the common law tradition of judicial review begun with Coke, it is right to conclude, as Blackstone does, that, "Upon the whole . . . we may take it as a general rule, 'that the decisions of courts of justice are the evidence of what is common law'" (1, Introduction, Section 3). Judges, even when striking down an act of Parliament, do not make law. Thus, it is not a single actor within government that makes the English model exceptional; it is the functioning of the whole that allows liberty to reign. Blackstone asserts that "the true excellence of the English government is that all the parts of it form a mutual check upon each other . . . every branch of our civil polity supports and is supported, regulates and is regulated, by the rest" (1. Chapter 2). To elaborate, Blackstone writes:

Like three distinct powers in mechanics, they jointly impel the machine of government in a direction different from what either, acting by themselves, would have done; but at the same time in a direction partaking of each, and formed out of all; a direction which constitutes the true line of liberty and happiness of the community. (1. Chapter 2)

Blackstone observes in the English system what the framers of the American Constitution adopted as their own.

Equally important to understanding Blackstone's common law is understanding his position on various procedural and substantive rights found at common law. While some may conclude, based on what was discussed earlier, that Blackstone departed greatly from the common law of Coke, they would be misguided. Not only does Blackstone follow in the common law tradition of fusing reason with custom, he also seeks out legal rights in traditional common law sources, including the Magna Carta. Like Coke, Blackstone found in the common law the preservation of individual liberties with respect to community needs. The common law provided the legal structure necessary for balancing these sometimes competing interests, while deferring to the individual when the conflict was irresolvable, as it was society that existed for the welfare of the individual, and not the other way around. "This is what we mean by the original contract of society . . . namely that the whole should protect its parts, and that every party should pay obedience to the will of the whole . . . the community should guard the rights of each individual . . . and that each individual should submit to the laws of the community. . . ." (1, Introduction, Section 2). Natural law provided the necessary out Blackstone was looking for when it came to granting the individual primacy in its relation to society. Natural rights were not alterable, and their preservation was the central purpose of organized society; and when human law conflicted with natural law, human law was not binding (1. Chapter 1). This is not authorization for lawlessness or an effort to reduce the authority of the state, but only an effort to guarantee that the presumption of liberty he found at common law was maintained.

The rights themselves thus defined by [the common law], consist in a number of private immunities; which will appear, from what has been premised, to be indeed no other, than either that residuum of natural liberty, which is not required by the laws of society to be sacrificed to public convenience; or else those civil privileges, which society hath engaged to provide, in lieu of the natural liberties so given up by individuals. These therefore were formerly, by inheritance or purchase, the rights of all mankind; but, in most other countries of the world being now more or less debased and destroyed, they at present may be said to remain, in a peculiar and emphatical manner, the rights of the people of England. And these may be reduced to three principal or primary articles; the right of personal security, the right of personal liberty; and the right of private property: because as there is no other known method of compulsion, or of abridging man's natural free will, but by an infringement or diminution of one or other of these important rights, the preservation of these, inviolate, may justly be said to include the preservation of our civil immunities in their largest and most extensive sense. (1. Chapter 1)

Thus, Blackstone—who is not alone on this matter—recognizes the need for government restriction on individual action in order to secure natural rights. But he also recognizes that the source of that protection can turn tyrannical if gone unchecked. While his thought will not be fully discussed until the next chapter, Blackstone captures vital aspects of John Locke's political theory. Like Locke, Blackstone recognizes that human existence in the absence of government leaves one's rights unsafe and susceptible to infringement. Therefore, in order to enjoy what is naturally theirs, individuals join into a government. Thus, the legitimacy of government only extends to its protection of individual rights. Once the government subverts its purpose and threatens the rights of individuals, the government is illegitimate. As James Ely writes, "Lockean theory also permeated English common law. In his *Commentaries on the Laws of England* William Blackstone built on Locke's formulation and defined property rights in sweeping terms. 'So great moreover . . . is the regard of the law for private property, that it will not authorize the least violation of it'" (Ely 1998, p. 17).[12] And as Albert Alschuler points out, "Blackstone, echoing Locke, declared that rights to personal security, liberty, and property were accorded by 'the immutable laws [of nature]'" (Alschuler 1996, p. 23).

Blackstone understood, as Locke did, that government grants people the security to develop their natural faculties, and through their developed faculties develop the world around them in ways that could not be done without government (2. Chapter 1). And, as it was man's natural condition to develop the land, his natural condition became threatened when the population grew and land became scarce. Such a development would necessarily lead to a rise in conflicts, thus making government necessary. But more than necessary, government allowed men the ability to work the land as they would not have to worry about defending it against attacks. Therefore, cultivated land led to the need of government, and government insured its continued existence (2. Chapter 1). For Blackstone, "Necessity begat property; and in order to ensure that property, recourse was had to civil society, which brought along with it a long train of inseparable concomitants—states, government, laws, punishments. . . ." (2. Chapter 1).

Men are endowed with three absolute rights: life, liberty, and property. The third absolute right, inherent in every Englishman, is that of property: which consists in the free use, enjoyment, and disposal of all his acquisitions without any control or diminution save only by the laws of the land. The original of private property is probably founded in nature, . . . but certainly the modifications under which we at present find it, the method of conserving it in the present owner, and of translating it from man to man are entirely derived from society and are some of those civil advantages in exchange for which every individual has resigned a part of his natural liberty. (1. Chapter 1)

The reader of this paragraph must be careful. It could be read to mean that because property as we know it is the product of society, then society can take property as we know it away from the individual whenever it so chooses. But this is not the point when read in context. Because the development and improvement of landed property in the state of nature was the natural course for man, society was created to allow man to continue to do what was natural in a safer environment. Therefore, to take away an individual's land would be to take away what is natural, in addition to violating the original intention of government. One need not look too far to see Blackstone make this point:

So great moreover, is the regard of the law of private property that it will not authorize the least violation of it; no, not even for the general good of the whole community. If a new road, for instance, were to be made through the grounds of a private person, it might perhaps be extensively beneficial to the public; but the law permits no man, or set of men, to do this without consent of the owner of the land. In vain may it be urged, that the good of the individual ought to yield to that of the community; for it would be dangerous to allow any private man, or even any public tribunal, to be the judge of this common good, and to decide whether it be expedient or not. (1. Chapter 1)

When referring to property, Blackstone is clear in what he means: "There is nothing which so generally strikes the imagination, and engages the affections of mankind, as the right of property; or that sole and despotic dominion which one man claims and exercises over the external things of the world, in total exclusion of the right of any other individual in the universe" (2. Section 2). And while it is helpful to have a precise definition, this definition does not help clear up some existing ambiguities about the relationship between the individual and the community when it comes to property. That is, even the most ardent supporter of property rights recognizes that, from time to time, taking or limiting man's property will be necessary for the continued security and perpetuation of the community. For instance, property owners could not engage in an activity with their property that would harm another. Such a restriction is found in natural law as well. But it is not until government enters the picture that one must worry about one's property being taken by the government for the good of the community. This is the question at the heart of the U.S. Supreme Court's takings jurisprudence. Fortunately, the members of the U.S. Supreme Court do not have to chart these waters alone, as Blackstone offers some insight into the proper balance between individual and society when it comes to property. Blackstone follows Coke's understanding of the law of the land and property seizure when he writes:

> It is enacted [by common law] that no man's lands or goods shall be seized into the king's hands, against the great charter, and the law of the land; and that no man shall be disinherited, nor put out of his franchises or freehold, unless he be duly brought to answer, and be forejudged by course of law; and if any thing be done to the contrary, it shall be redressed, and holden for none. (1. Chapter 1)

Therefore, government cannot arbitrarily take land from an individual; it must adhere to due process of the law. One restriction on government taking is that the government must pay the citizen for his property. That is, the government cannot take property "by absolutely stripping the subject of his property in an arbitrary manner; but by giving him a full indemnification and equivalent for the injury thereby sustained," which means "the law of the land has postponed even public necessity to the sacred and inviolable rights of private property" (1. Chapter 1). But Blackstone understands this to be a greater protection on property rights than modern readers do, as he understands due process of law to mean more than just compensation (1. Chapter 1). Like Coke before him, Blackstone understood the due process protections found at common law, specifically chapter 29 of the Magna Carta 1225, to mean that the forfeiture of property, or the deprivation of any economic right, could only be done when the owner was brought to answer under due process of law. Due process of law means, "by indictment or presentment of good and lawful men where such deeds be done in due manner, or by writ original of the common law" (1, Introduction, Section 3).

When taken as a whole, Blackstone's thought is both original and traditional. He looks to strengthen the place of the judiciary within the English model of his time, and he looks to bring greater certainty to the law in order to grant greater protections to members of society. In some respects, he is caught between Hobbes's positivism and Coke's artificial reason. What Blackstone adds is a systematic assessment of rights and the limitation placed on government by the law that goes missing in Coke. While Coke recognizes that there are limitations to government, he does not offer a systematic account of what those limitations are, nor offer a theoretical justification for those limitations. Blackstone remedies this deficiency in Coke's thought. One might worry that Blackstone is setting himself up for failure in that he has created a government stronger than Coke's and thereby given it the strength to threaten individual rights. But, by clearly stating what rights individuals retain, and those that are off limits to government infringement, Blackstone gives the judiciary the power to thwart the tyranny of the majority. The question that remains, however, is whether the judicial activism advocated by Blackstone can be taken in a direction even he did not desire. It seems there must be an equilibrium between Coke and Hobbes that Blackstone tries to find. Unfortunately, this book will not exhaust the debate over the success or failure of Blackstone's mission.

IV. AMERICAN ADAPTATION

The influences on American law are numerous, but this book seeks to isolate the two most important in terms of understanding rights: English common law and John Locke. Chapters 3–4 give an in-depth examination of American governing documents, which will provide evidence for the previously stated thesis. This section is only intended to provide some preliminary evidence to show the infusion of common law into the American legal tradition in order to provide a framework for the following chapters.

While it may be difficult to show Locke's influence on the founding because there is some contention over how much influence Locke had on the thinking of American colonists, trying to demonstrate the influence of the common law is much less difficult given that the American colonists were raised under the English system and brought it with them to the states. What is less clear is which parts of the common law remained in the American psyche after the Revolution. This chapter suggests that the conception of rights and the government's role in preserving those rights as expressed in Coke and Blackstone remained with Americans even after the Revolution. As Donald Lutz shows, Blackstone and Coke were two of the most cited thinkers in eighteenth-century America.[13] But given the complexity of their thought and the multitude of topics the common law incorporates, we must go beyond Lutz to see whether the common law conception of rights made it into the American legal tradition. As Paul Reinsch makes clear, in part by quoting Joseph Story:

> Statutory law making had but sparingly been used up to this time in England, and the law of property and personal security, criminal law, and procedure, found their norms in a long series of judicial precedents. The transfer of this system to the colonies . . . constitutes a subject of rare interest. . . . The accepted legal theory of this transfer is well known. It is clearly stated by Story in *Van Ness v. Packard*, 2 Peters, 144: "The common law of England is not to be taken in all respects to be that of America. Our ancestors brought with them

its general principles, and claimed it as their birth right, but they brought with them and adopted only that portion which was applicable to their condition." (Reinsch 1970, p. 6)

Therefore, I will begin to show in this section what will be concluded in the following chapters, that the American conception of rights, specifically property rights, is a unique fusion of Enlightenment philosophy and common law ideals. Americans drew on both sources to strengthen the common law conception of rights that would then allow them to adopt a higher-law understanding of rights that was grounded in custom and history yet independent of England's custom and history.

What has earlier been alluded to deserves some elaboration and outside confirmation. Because most of the American colonies were initially chartered and settled during the early seventeenth century when Coke's career as a judge and member of Parliament was at its height, Coke exerted a comparable influence on colonial law. A large number of seventeenth century American lawyers received their legal education in England, where Coke's *Reports* and *Institutes* were a staple of legal education. Moreover, English books on law and political theory were readily available in America throughout the seventeenth and eighteenth centuries and again, especially Coke's *Reports* and *Institutes,* which were widely read in the colonies and were by far their most authoritative law texts until the publication of Blackstone's *Commentaries* in 1765. (Gedicks 2008, p. 44)

Just as important as the legal education Americans received from Coke's writings was their political education. As discussed earlier, Coke established a political theory that subjected everyone to the law, even the Crown and Parliament. It was Coke who argued that a law in violation of reason is no law at all. The Americans adopted this view, in conjunction with others, to give legitimacy to their revolutionary claims. They felt that a number of English laws violated those rights that were found at common law, and because they considered themselves English subjects who should enjoy the law of the land as expressed by Coke, which he adopted from the Magna Carta, they were justified in rejecting those laws. When their rights, as they understood them, were violated, they went to Coke for a higher-law constitutionalism that justified their grievances and their claim that Parliament's laws were in fact no laws at all. "Coke's reading of substance into due process was adopted by the American colonies and adapted to their struggle against Britain in the 1760s and 1770s. . . . The eighteenth century American adoption of seventeenth century English higher-law constitutionalism is the necessary backdrop for the argument that the doctrine of substantive due process was within the original understanding of the Fifth Amendment" (Geddicks 2008, p. 15). Thus, as already stated, the conception of rights found at common law found its way into the American colonies and was adopted by the colonies in their move toward independence and taken up again when drafting and ratifying the Constitution and Bill of Rights.

Of course, Coke was not the only common law thinker the Americans knew. According to Albert Alschuler, Blackstone was the author of the most influential law book in late eighteenth-century America. Alschuler states that, "all of our formative documents . . . were drafted by attorneys steeped in Blackstone's *Commentaries*" (Alschuler 1996, p. 2).[14] And while the first American edition of the *Commentaries* did not appear until 1772, there already had been 1,000 copies of the English edition sold in the colonies prior to this date. This fact, and others, has led scholars like Daniel Boorstin to write, "in the history of American institutions, no other book . . . has played so great a role" (Boorstin 1958, p. 3).

However, given the immense scope of both Coke's and Blackstone's writing, it must be more clearly stated what it was the Americans took from each of these thinkers. For Bernard Siegan, it is clear which part of Coke and Blackstone the Americans adopted as their own:

> The commentaries on Chapter 39[15] by Coke and Blackstone rejected the position that the due process guarantee (as distinguished from the concept) related only to procedure. Both regarded it as the fundamental provision protecting individual liberties. The American legal community, which played a critical role in the framing and ratifying of the Constitution and Bill of Rights, considered both men to be leading authorities on English law and was greatly influenced by them. The common understanding is vital to interpreting the due process clauses in American federal and state constitutions. . . . Based on its legal heritage, which encompasses Chapter 39 of the Magna Carta and the commentaries of Locke, Coke, and Blackstone, the due process guarantee is at the root of a society founded on individual autonomy and dignity. Persons who abide by the law and do not inflict harm should be safe in their persons and possessions from deprivation by government. . . . Thus, interpreting the Fifth Amendment's due process clause requires distinguishing between the due process concept and the due process clause guaranteeing it. . . . The clause is a restraint on government, prohibiting any branch of it from depriving people of life, liberty, or property without fair and proper judicial processes and proceedings. (Siegan 1997, p. 24)

A similar point is repeated by Ely who writes that partly because of Blackstone's influence, "To the colonial mind, property and liberty were inseparable, as evidenced by the colonists' willingness to break with England when the mother country seemingly threatened property ownership" (Ely 1998, p. 17).

By a conservative estimate, five of the ten amendments that compose the Bill of Rights have direct ties to the Magna Carta. The prohibition of quartering soldiers (Amendment III, Magna Carta chapters 19, 20, and 21); protections against unlawful searches and seizures (Amendment IV, Magna Carta chapter 29); due process and property provisions (Amendment V, Magna Carta chapters 8, 19, 20, 21, and 29); right to trial by jury (Amendment VII, Magna Carta chapters 14, 17, and 29); and protections against excessive bail and fines (Amendment VIII, Magna Carta chapters 8 and 29). In fact, Willmoore Kendall suggests that the Bill of Rights is simply common-law specificities (Kendall 1971, p. 12). While he is perhaps accurate, I have only included those provisions that can be traced directly to the Magna Carta.

For the purposes of this book, those provisions at common law and in the American Constitution that apply to property are the most important. To appreciate what the framers and ratifiers of the Fifth Amendment meant by property, it is important to know what the common law meant by property and its protection through law. As was seen in the earlier discussion, property refers most often to landed estate, and its protection can only be compromised if the survival of the society depends upon it, as property without government is not secure and thus depends on society to make it secure. While Locke, Blackstone, and the American founders, specifically Madison, give a richer—and dual—definition of property, their view of its purpose and relationship between individual and society remains the same. While the rest of the book draws on a number of writings from American scholars, jurists and politicians to make this point, it is appropriate to reference Chancellor Kent in particular. In his *Commentaries on American Law,* he argues that property leads to increased levels of comfort, useful arts, charity, benevolent affections, and taste for the finer things in life. For Kent, as it was for Blackstone and Coke, property is inherent and natural to man, which makes it an unalienable right (Kent 1836, Vol. 2, p. 340–347). Kent writes:

> The words, "law of the land," as used originally in Magna Carta, in reference to this subject, are understood to mean, due process of law, that is, by indictment or presentment of good and lawful men: "and this," says Lord Coke, "is the true sense and exposition of these words." (Kent 1836, Vol. 2, p. 13)

Because these rights were paramount to the colonial and revolutionary generations—and those that closely followed—Americans felt justified in breaking with England when its King and Parliament threatened these rights. And while the common law gave great authority to tradition, custom, and the rule of law, it also granted a higher status to rights. This meant that when the government failed to act in accord with rights, its law failed to achieve the status of law. This has lead Michael Zuckert to write, "Partly because of him [Blackstone], the Americans could at once think of political society as the rationalist product of a social compact and as an entity shaped and governed by a law built on custom, deriving its authority from its antiquity and 'grown' character" (Zuckert 2002, p. 240).

Americans adopted the common law theme of rights. At common law, rights were limits placed upon the government for the purpose of preserving life, liberty, and property. It was the triad that gave procedural rights their importance, for without life, liberty, and property there would be no reason to have a law of the land. But equally important, it was through the triad that other rights could be preserved. Life, liberty, and property are at once the ends and the means. The triad has both instrumental and intrinsic value. This is why I argue that there is a unity of rights.

Chapters 3 and 4 of this book will show specific instances of where American colonial and postcolonial charters and constitutions rephrased many of the common law due process principles. It is enough for this chapter to simply put forward the argument and some evidence that the common law had a profound influence on the American founding, so that when the reader gets to the later chapters, the proper groundwork has already been laid.

NOTES

1. See Ober (2006) for an argument of why self-rule should be considered an intrinsic value. I argue that due process rights can possess intrinsic value.

2. At the time, there was no distinction between substantive and procedural due process rights. This did not come until the New Deal of the United States. One reason I use the terms *intrinsic* and *instrumental* is so I can avoid any confusion that might be associated with the post–New Deal understanding of substantive and procedural due process rights.

3. The Magna Carta is the perfect metaphor for common law origin on whole, given that it was founded in an attempt to bring every member of society, even the King, under the rule of law, and it is relied on as a source of authority, though its legal meaning was constantly evolving through statute and precedent to meet the changing societal demands. But, never lost was its authority, partly because of its adaptability, and partly because of its obscure origin. As Stoner writes of Coke, "Coke recognizes that the obscurity of the origin of the common law is in some respects the secret of its success: It makes the law in its most fundamental points unwritten and thus leaves it always dependent upon reason for its discovery, confirmation, and elaboration" (Stoner 1992, p. 67).

4. Both sets of rights, intrinsic and instrumental, confer legitimacy upon government because the preservation of each is the purpose for government. The presence of each is what makes the rule of law valuable and possible. When government is absent, or when there is tyranny, the presence of intrinsic and instrumental rights is unreliable. Instrumental rights are needed to protect intrinsic rights, and therefore must be the foundation of government procedures and institutions. In addition, instrumental rights prevent a move toward anarchy just as intrinsic rights prevent a move toward tyranny. To sacrifice instrumental rights for intrinsic rights would make intrinsic rights insecure in the long run. To do the reverse would render instrumental rights meaningless. Neither intrinsic nor instrumental rights can exist at the expense of the other.

5. This understanding of rights is repeated throughout the rest of the book as I characterize property rights as both procedural and substantive rights.

6. While both Stoner and Scott reach some agreement on this point, they disagree about what it was Coke and the American founders had in mind.

7. This type of practical reasoning is generally referred to as *phronesis*.

8. The accounts of the three takings cases decided by Coke are adapted from Siegan (2001), p. 25–27. *Mouse's Case* is also adapted from the same source.

9. This bears directly upon my analysis of the *Berman, Parker,* and *Kelo* in chapter 5 as none of the improvements to be carried out were done by a government agent, but private entities, and in no instance were the improvements—with perhaps one exception—necessary for the survival of the community. Coke's decision also shows that courts have not always deferred to the legislative branch on matters relating to the public good and economic policy.

10. While I have argued elsewhere that Blackstone is more consistent with Enlightenment thinkers than the common law on matters relating to the role of the judiciary (Scott 2008), I will here argue that Blackstone's adherence to the common law's understanding of property is consistent with Coke's, but becomes more focused as a result of his Enlightenment influences.

11. All references to Blackstone are to *Commentaries on the Laws of England* unless specifically noted otherwise. The references are to volume and section number. In most instances, spelling and punctuation has been edited to conform to modern readership expectations.

12. Ely has recently released a third edition of his book on property rights. This is fortunate as the discipline needs as many clear-thinking commentators as it can get when it comes to property rights. This book departs from Ely's efforts by placing greater emphasis on the political and philosophical dimensions of the property rights debate. Also, this book provides an original critique of the Court's reasoning in *Kelo*.

13. Blackstone was second, and Coke was tenth on the list. John Locke came in at number three.

14. At this point, Alschuler is quoting Robert A. Ferguson's *Law and Letters in American Culture,* p. 11 (1984).

15. Remember, chapter 39 of the 1215 charter becomes chapter 29 of the 1225 iteration.

Chapter 2

Locke on Property

This chapter does not set out to settle the debate over John Locke's influence on the American founding. While worthwhile, that topic has received extensive coverage from a number of qualified commentators with whom I do not seek to quarrel (Pangle 1988; Banning 1978; Pocock 1975; Bailyn 1967; Hartz 1955; Becker 1942; Beard 1913). Instead, the objective of this chapter is more limited: to explicate clearly what Locke said about property. The assumption is that understanding what Locke had to say about property will bring us closer to an understanding of the Constitution's position on property rights. This chapter will provide a close reading of the *Second Treatise* that will result in a clear and straightforward understanding of Locke's teaching on property. Some have suggested that understanding Locke's teaching on property is the key to unlocking his entire political philosophy (Strauss 1953). While this is not a point I dispute, I think it is necessary to provide an adequate account of Locke's theory of property before such a conclusion is reached. This attempt distinguishes itself from previous attempts in that it provides a systematic account of the doctrine's development independent of his other teachings. Moreover, this account departs from the orthodox readings of Locke (Sabine 1961). My account of Locke demonstrates that the end of government is the preservation of property, as it is through the preservation of property that men can escape a violent and destitute existence.

The nominal purpose of chapter V in the *Second Treatise* is to show how men came to have a right to property. The chapter traces property's development from God's gift to all mankind to the protection of which being the proper end of government. But understanding the beginning and ending is insufficient, and analysis of the development of Locke's argument yields difficult puzzles and nuances that must be addressed to understand the full implication of the conclusion Locke reaches. This chapter traces Locke's account of how man acquires property, the changes that result from the introduction of money, and the relationship between property and government.

I. THE INITIAL ACCOUNT OF HOW MAN ACQUIRES PROPERTY

In the first section of chapter V, Locke tries to convince the reader that whether the reader relies on reason or revelation, he or she can reach the conclusion that the world was given to mankind[1] in common (§25).[2] While Locke cites Biblical Scripture—at this point Psalms CXV.16—thus demonstrating that the right to acquire property is grounded in revelation, it is not until he stops quoting the Bible that he concludes that God has "given it to mankind in common" (§25).[3]

In the next section, Locke seems to restate his previous point—without referencing Scripture this time—but he drops revelation from the manner in which we come to know man's right to property and refers to reason alone (§26). According to Locke, man has property in himself, and when he mixes his labor with something that lay in common in nature, he has taken it out of its natural state and it becomes his by virtue of mixing his labor with it (§27). To be sure, the moment he takes it out of its natural state, not when he cooks it or eats it, it becomes his, and if not then, then never (§28, §29).[4] But man may not take more than he can use (§31). While his famous definition of property that is paraphrased by Thomas Jefferson in the *U.S. Declaration of Independence* is not given until §87, in chapter VII, Locke tells us at §32 that the chief matter of property is the earth itself, not the fruits of the earth or the beasts that subsist on it.[5]

Beyond assertions and misquotations of scripture, Locke's teaching in the first seven sections of chapter V does not rest on very much. Beginning at §32, Locke provides a more substantial defense of private property. In this section, and repeated in §35, we see that man cultivates the land because he must. In some sense, Locke now returns to Scripture—without quoting—to show that God commanded man to labor, and it is because of the penury of his condition that he must work the land. What Locke fails to mention is that God only commanded man to labor after the Fall, and that Adam originally had no need to cultivate the land.[6]

At §34 we again see Locke say that God has given the earth to all man in common, a point similarly made at §§25–26 and §31. But this time Locke conditions the statement even more than he does at §26. Now Locke says that even if given in common, there is no way God intended for it to remain in common and uncultivated, but instead gave it to the rational and industrious so that they could cultivate it. His reasoning draws on the point made at §32 and §35 that God commanded man to labor. That is, according to Locke, we know that God wanted us to cultivate the land because he told us to. Therefore, those who will cultivate the land are those to whom God truly gave the land. Coupling this with the fact that man has possession over his labor (§27), Locke brings us closer to his defense of private property. This point is forcefully made when Locke writes, "From all which it is evident, that though the things of nature are given in common, yet man, being master of himself,[7] and *proprietor of his own person, and the actions or labour of it, had still in himself the great foundation of property;* and that, which made up the great part of what he applied to the support or comfort of his being, when invention and arts had improved the conveniences of life, was perfectly his own, and did not belong in common to others" (§44, italics are Locke's).

§44 relies on a premise that has not yet been explored. Locke argues that nature alone furnishes only the worthless materials to man, and nature becomes useful when man mixes his labor with nature (§26, §37, §40, §42, §43). In fact, the man who cultivates land increases its worth one hundred times over its original value (§37). Locke goes on to say in this section that a man who cultivates land gives ninety-nine times more to mankind than does nature alone. Locke shifts his position on cultivating—or possibly adds—from a necessity to a good. That is, in §37, the reader does not see Locke treating work as something man was commanded to do, or must do, but it is something that improves mankind.[8]

Therefore, Locke sets up a scenario in which man's labor has value, man is the proprietor of his own labor, objects in nature do not have value, and man must—and should—cultivate nature; therefore, mixing one's labor with nature makes whatever man takes out of its natural state his own.

II. MONEY

The previous section left off with a summary of Locke's argument for property. §39, and repeated at §51, provides a concise summary of §§25–38 and seems to conclude the task Locke sets out for himself at the beginning of chapter V; but there remain twelve sections after §39, but only eleven introduce something new. §§40–50 discuss what is left out of Locke's summary of his teaching at §39 and §51, specifically, the limit on man's right to acquire and the increase in the world's supply of goods through labor.[9]

It is important to remember that at §31 Locke introduces the spoilage rule. This rule simply states that man may not take more than he can use for God did not create anything to spoil or be destroyed (§31, §37).[10] §§36–37 introduce the concept of money, but it is not until §50 that Locke discusses the full import of money.[11] In all sections that discuss money, it is agreed that the value of money comes through consent. Gold has no intrinsic value, but when men agree that it is worth something, they trade goods for it; and man can hoard as much gold as he would like because, unlike apples, gold does not spoil. The introduction of money, which is based upon man's reason and ingenuity, allows man to circumvent the spoilage rule.

Money comes prior to civil society (§50). But more important than the timeline is the implication of money for pre-civil and civil society. With the introduction of money, "men have agreed to a disproportionate and unequal *possession of the earth,* they having, by receiving in exchange for the overplus gold and silver, which may be hoarded up without injury to any one. . . . This partage of things in an inequality of private possessions, men have made practicable out of the bounds of society, and without compact. . . ." (§50, Locke's italics). For pre-civil society, it is clear that Locke thinks labor gives man right to property, but once money is introduced, it gives man right to property as well. The introduction of money, and the role it plays in pre-civil society, is paramount for understanding Locke's theory of property ownership in civil society.

II A. Man Enlarges Possessions

Money allowed man to circumvent the spoilage rule. Subsequently, man began to enlarge his possessions (§§48–49). Because money does not spoil, man—with the invention of money—is able to enlarge his possessions without violating the original limitation on his urge to acquire (§46).

Locke considers this process natural, or at least intrinsic to man's nature. "Find out something that hath the *use and value of money* amongst his neighbours, you shall see the same man will begin presently to enlarge his possessions" (§49, Locke's italics). The preceding section makes the same point when Locke argues that if you isolate man from commerce, in a setting in which he has plenty and no resources for creating money, he will not work to enlarge his possessions (§48). Man living within a reasonable proximity to others in which they can partake in commerce and have consented to the use of money, will be further encouraged to cultivate the land in order to enlarge his stores of money, and not just land (§42). And because it is man's labor that provides land with its greatest value, this sort of system ought to be encouraged (§42). Money seems to be the mechanism by which man pursues his urge to acquire; it does not instill in him the urge, for if there was no urge originally then money would not have been invented (§48).[12]

Man's acquisition does not add just to his own stock, but adds to the entire community's. At §37 we see that when man cultivates one acre of land, he contributes an additional ninety-nine acres worth of goods above what nature would have provided on its own. Man can make one acre produce what nature alone would have produced with one hundred.[13] This excess is exchanged either in a barter system or sold once money has been invented. Once money has been invented, and thus the spoilage rule circumvented, mankind has an incentive for cultivating the land. Therefore, with the invention of money, the material possessions increase (§42, §45, §48). And with the increase in material possessions, there is an increase in population (§45).

With the introduction of money, land will also become scarce, as man will seek to enlarge his possession of land (§36, §45).[14] As one man enlarges his land, he limits the amount of land available to others. And because the spoilage rule no longer applies, he can use as much land as he can do so productively. Man is limited by more than just the spoilage rule, it seems, because no man will seek to enlarge his possessions if he cannot benefit materially from the enlargement (§§48–49). Therefore, no man will fence in and claim for his own more land than he can cultivate, nor does he have the right to, even absent the spoilage rule (§34). Man has physical limitations that would limit the amount of land he can cultivate on his own. But after the introduction of money, a man may employ others to cultivate his land for him (§85). Thus, money allows man to overcome not only the spoilage rule, but also his own physical limitations. After the introduction of money, the intrinsic value of things is altered, and labor alone no longer grants title to property.

II B. Inequality Results

To briefly summarize, those things given to man by nature are nearly worthless without man's labor (§§41–43). Once man mixes his labor with it, he increases the value of that which is given to him by nature (§37, §40, §§42–43).[15] Man is able, through his ingenuity, to circumvent the spoilage rule by introducing money, which then allows him to increase his possessions and material wealth (§§36–37, §§45–47). Land becomes scarce as a result, but it has also become more valuable because of man (§36, §45, §50).

Locke makes it clear that his use of equality is qualified: "Though I have said above that all men by nature are equal, I cannot be supposed to understand all sorts of equality. . . ." (§54). Some men are unequal through birth, merit, age, physical nature, or perhaps even intelligence. In fact, we know that all men have reason, but it is by choice that they use it (§6). And in chapter V the reader sees that some men are rational and industrious whereas others are quarrelsome and contentious (§34). So it seems logical, if not natural, that with the introduction of money, there will continue to be inequality, but this time it is in terms of material possession, which was impossible before by virtue of the spoilage rule.

The introduction of money occurs prior to, or at least outside of, civil society (§50). This raises the question of what ought to be done about property ownership and the resulting inequality after civil society is formed. In light of §48, and what has been said previously about nature providing the worthless materials and man providing the value to nature, which increases our standard of living that results, we might conclude that at a minimum civil society must be structured in a way that preserves the incentives for productivity that man has created outside of civil society (§48, §108).

III. END OF GOVERNMENT AS IT RELATES TO PROPERTY

The purpose of creating laws and constitutions is to protect property (§30, §50).[16] While this may appear too narrow, remember that for Locke property is inextricably linked to liberty (§12, §18, §42, §50). Property ownership originates within man's self, of which he alone is master (§27, §44)[17]; man's possessions—and their size—are derivative of him because he has property in himself, and by extension it is in those things he mixes his labor with that had previously lain in common (§6, §48, §50); government is instituted to protect property (§6, §34, §42, §50, §54).[18] Thus, for Locke, property is the material manifestation of one's right.[19] Locke explicitly references private property— and the resulting scarcity—as a right (§36). Because man has an exclusive claim to himself—and thus his labor—he has an exclusive claim to those things he mixes his labor with, thus granting him a right to those things, which another cannot take away without his consent (§26, §34). The transformation of property into something useful, and appropriation of property among men after it has been transformed, is carried out by man prior to government.

Property has a dual meaning for Locke, but the two meanings are interconnected. While the chief matter of property is land, the value of the land that man has mixed his labor with is derived from the property, which each man possesses within himself. This point is clearly made by Locke at §27 and §44. "The claim to property in one's own person is thus simply central to Locke's enterprise. . . . The earth and all the lower animals are 'common,' yet the human person is property of the human self, that is, private to themselves, possessing a claim of right not to be interfered with" (Zuckert 1994, p. 276, 277). The reason man's labor gives him right to those things in which he mixes it with, what previously lay in common, is that man has property in himself.[20] Therefore, when Locke tells us that the protection of property is the end of government, he is referring both to external property and that property man possesses within himself. Just for good measure, should someone think that what Locke writes in the *Second Treatise* is an aberration, what he writes in *A Letter Concerning Toleration* is wholly consistent with what has been said up to this point[21]:

> The commonwealth seems to me to be a society of men constituted only for the procuring, preserving, and advancing their own civil interests. Civil interest I call life, liberty, health, and indolency of body; and the possession of outward things, such as money, lands, houses, furniture, and the like. . . . [T]he necessity of preserving men in the possession of what honest industry has already acquired, and also of preserving their liberty and strength, whereby they may acquire what they farther want, obliges men to enter into society with one another; that by mutual assistance and joint force, they may secure unto each other their properties, in the things that contribute to the comforts and happiness of this life . . . it is easy to understand to what end the legislative power ought to be directed . . . and that is the temporal good and outward prosperity of society, which is the sole reason of men's entering into society, and the only thing they seek and aim at in it. . . . (Locke 2003, p. 218 and 242–243)

The protection of landed property gains its normative justification in Locke because landed property is derived from the property man has within himself. The property man has within himself is his life and liberty, or those things that form the basis of his natural rights. Therefore, secure landed property is the result of man living in a condition in which his life and liberty are secure, thus natural rights are not at risk in a government that protects property.

Locke does not make light of the necessity to protect property. "[T]he right of employing them [lands and men], is the great art of government: and that prince, who shall be so wise and godlike, as by established law of liberty to secure protection and encouragement to the honest industry of mankind, against the oppression of power and narrowness of party, will quickly be too hard for his neighbours . . ." (§42).[22] Just as forcefully, Locke states earlier in chapter V that it is the civilized part of mankind that has formed positive laws to determine property as consistent with the original natural order (§30). And if the reader is still in doubt after chapter V, as to what the role of government is, Locke clears the matter up when he writes, "whereas government has no other end but the preservation of property" (§94) and again when he writes, "The reason why men enter into society, is the preservation of their property; and why they chuse and authorize a legislative, is, that there may be laws made, and rules set, as guards and

fences to the properties of all the members of the society. . . ." (§222).[23]
And, if the government fails to provide this service, man may dissolve the
government (Chapter XIX).[24]

If man is not secure in his property, he is not secure in his person (§12,
§18). Property is the result of man. Therefore, to deprive man of his property
is to deprive him of what he has created through that which he alone is master. To take away his property is to deprive him of his labor, or in the case of
a society that has created money, his ingenuity.[25] In either instance, property
and right are synonymous, as one's liberty and safety are limited when one's
property is limited. Therefore, in order to be legitimate, and to achieve the
goal man left the state of nature to pursue, government must protect property.
This conclusion rests on the assumption that man left the state of nature
because the state of nature was unfit to protect man's property. If this can be
shown, then the conclusion can be reached that the reason why government
must protect property is that the only reason—or at least the primary reason—
man created government was to escape a condition in which property was not
secure. Unless this can be shown, all the reader has is a series of propositions
that demonstrate property is good and therefore government ought to protect
it. And while this may be compelling enough, it does not confront the complexity of Locke's argument.

The conclusion that the end of government is to protect property assumes
that the state of nature is not a state of peace. There is perhaps no other topic
in the *Second Treatise* that gives rise to more conflict among scholars than
the various states that existed before man entered into civil society (Zuckert
1994; Pangle 1988; Ashcraft 1986; Tully 1980; Sabine 1961; Strauss 1953).
When read in the context of the end of government and the discussion of
property, it seems clear that the state of nature is not a peaceful place, and
is closer to the state of war—if not indistinguishable from—than commonly
assumed.

Locke's state of nature causes disagreement among readers because quite
early in the *Second Treatise* we see Locke discuss the state of nature as perfect freedom and equality (§4) but then go on to show that the freedom one
possesses in this state is qualified (§4, §6) just as equality is qualified (§54).
In addition to the state of nature, Locke introduces the state of war and the
state of peace. Locke sets up a scenario in which the state of nature and the
state of war are as far distant as a state of peace and a state of enmity (§19).
What some commentators have suggested is that the state of war and the state
of peace are at opposite ends of the spectrum, and the state of nature falls
somewhere in between (Sabine 1961). This conclusion rests on something
other than a close reading of the section. All Locke admits at this point is
that the state of nature and the state of peace are equidistant from the state of

war, which leaves open the possibility that the state of nature and the state of peace are at the poles bisected by the state of war. Both charts would be an accurate representation of what Locke says at §19. The competing interpretations require the reader to look elsewhere if she or he is to understand the relationship between the state of war and the state of nature.

Man has certain fundamental rights in the state of nature (§6, §7, §8, §10, §11, §12, §16). On the surface, this appears to be positive, but when read closely, the enumerated rights in the state of nature are all rights man would exercise only if his security was challenged—such as the right to preserve one's life, the right to reparation, the right to kill murderers and lesser offenders. That is, the rights one has in the state of nature can be exercised only if the state of nature were one of conflict.

When men live together according to reason and without a common judge on earth, men are in a state of nature (§19). But men do not have to live according to reason nor consult reason. The use of reason is optional (§6, §19). Perhaps this is why in later sections Locke drops reason from the discussion and characterizes the state of nature as the lack of a common judge on earth (§87, §89). Even when Locke lists the three things commonwealths provide that are left wanting in the state of nature, a common judge on earth is the only one carried from §19 to §125. And in fact, even in the list of three, the other two hinge on there being a common judge on earth. The state of war may exist with or without a common judge as it is defined by the use of force without right (§19). But to determine right, there must be common judge on earth, for without one, men are left to be judges in their own case, and man will always be biased to himself and his interests (§13). At §13 Locke appears to attribute all the inconveniences found in the state of nature—"which must certainly be great" (§13)—to the lack of a common judge on earth, as there is no mention of reason or the other remedies introduced at §125. It appears from these comments that conflict will result when there is no common judge on earth, which makes it difficult for the reader to distinguish between the state of war and the state of nature except for the nominal difference that there is force without right—nominal because force without right seems inevitable when there is no common judge on earth—in the state of war.

At some point, man's property becomes "very unsafe, very unsecure" (§123) in the state of nature, which is why men are quickly driven into civil society (§127). When man's property is not secure, he is not secure (§12, §18). What caused the transition from a tranquil state of nature to one of turmoil is not spelled out by Locke, nor can it be definitively concluded. But what can be concluded is that when money was introduced, man had more to lose—and hence more to gain by using force without right against another man—which made his property less secure than it had been previously.

Because in the beginning men had little property, and thus little covetousness, he had less to fear (§75, §107). While the world was provided, at least initially, to man in common, it was only given to the rational and industrious who would cultivate and improve it through their labor to increase the comfort and support for man (§6, §26, §34, §54). This assumes, as Locke shows, that what nature provides is insufficient for man (§42, §43). This being the case, God commanded man to work the land (§32). But even this command loses its force when the reader finishes the sentence and realizes that man had no choice in the matter given the "penury of his condition" (§32). It seems odd to consider nature a gift from God if it required labor to give it value. But more than being required to do something because his existence depended upon it, man was inclined to do these things—both of which, however, make the creation of property natural for man. For without this inclination, there is no other way money would have been invented. Man, when put into a situation in which he lives with others in which the natural materials do not provide for his well-being, will work the land to improve his condition beyond that which is only necessary to feed, clothe, and shelter him (§42, §48, §49). Because of man's desire to increase his possessions, which was limited by the spoilage rule, man created money. With money, which was created independent of civil society (§50), came a new arrangement that allowed man to move beyond the spoilage rule and the condition in which labor alone granted right to property. Money allowed man to escape his penury condition as money allowed man to hoard property (§48) and enlarge his possessions (§49), which created a scarcity of land (§45)—which is "the chief matter of property" (§32). And while these were positive developments because they gave to mankind one hundred times more than nature could in terms of quantity and quality (§37, §40), it is clear that not everyone gained equally, which meant a new set of passions were introduced—vain ambition, insolence, covetousness, and luxury—that exposed man's insecurity and need for government (§107, §111). In order to secure his possessions and his safety against those who were not industrial or rational, and instead "desired the benefit of another's pains which he had no right to" (§34), man was "quickly driven into society" (§127).

It is only now that the reader can fully understand Locke's claim throughout the *Second Treatise* that the end of government is the protection of property. "Safety, ease, and plenty" come from man only after he has combined civil society with the more necessary arts (§101). It is only through government—whose greatest art is "the increase of lands and the right of employing them" (§42)—that man can avoid the state of war and the state of penury.[26]

IV. SUMMARY

In the following chapters the reader will see Locke's understanding of property, and the end of government as it relates to property, reflected in colonial charters and state constitutions that were established prior to the ratification of the Constitution and immediately after. The reader will also see how closely Madison's thought reflects Locke's in terms of property and the end of government.

Even those who argue that Locke did not have a direct influence on the thought of the founding generation cannot deny the relevant parallels between Locke's teaching on property and the treatment of property by the founding generation. Locke, even if not a direct influence on the founding, can sharpen our understanding of the founding generation as Locke provides a teaching of property that is seen throughout the revolutionary and founding periods. It is not for me to argue that Locke directly influenced those who drafted and ratified the Constitution and Bill of Rights. My purpose is less ambitious; I simply want to show the parallels between one of the most influential property rights philosophers and the American founding in order to articulate to the reader the functional and normative importance of property so that we may more clearly understand those principles behind the words in the Constitution, which will then aid us in pursuing a faithful reading of the document.

NOTES

1. I use *man* and *mankind* throughout this chapter when referring to Locke's words, even though using *human* and *humankind* would be more appropriate. The idea is to keep consistent with Locke's terminology so that a faithful reading of Locke can be achieved. Even on small matters, mixing terms can lead to a misrepresentation of the author's ideas.

2. All references to the *Second Treatise* are to the Macpherson 1980 edition cited in the bibliography.

3. It is not uncommon for Locke to misquote scripture or to begin with a scriptural quote and then end in his own words, on this point in particular see §6, §26, §31, §42, §50. Moreover, this statement, if taken in context of what Locke says of Filmer in the *First Treatise* and summarizes in §1 of the *Second Treatise,* the reader sees Locke potentially setting up an argument against a right to property based on God's granting it to man.

4. Zuckert properly characterizes labor as transformative and appropriating. Labor transforms what lay unclaimed in nature into property, and it appropriates it to the one who mixes his labor with it (Zuckert 1994, p. 278).

5. It will be discussed in greater detail later that the term *property* is broader than this section initially indicates.

6. §32 raises at least one interesting possibility that I will raise but not address as it is outside the scope of this text. If it is true that Locke is only speaking of man after

the Fall then we must recognize this as such and use it to interpret Locke's account of the state of nature as man, as considered by Locke, is someone who knows good and evil and thus a fallen creature. This could possibly negate any reading of the *Second Treatise* that equates the state of peace with the state of nature.

7. Locke leaves unanswered how it is possible for man to be his own master and yet be commanded by a higher force to do something.

8. If nature is provided by God, and man is his own master (§44), and man increases the value of those things God gave, what is Locke saying about God? Consider §42: "He will then see how much *labour makes the far greatest part of the value of things we enjoy in this world. . . . Land that is uncultivated is waste*" (§42, Locke's italics). This thought will be completed in the final section of this chapter.

9. There are sixteen sections that are directed at Locke's initial purpose for chapter V (§§25–39 and §51), which leaves eleven sections remaining in chapter V (§§40–50). God is mentioned sixteen times in the first eleven sections and not once in the last sixteen sections. This is not critical for my reading of Locke but might still be of interest to some. This is also the proper place to refer the reader to Zuckert 1994, p. 247–248 and mention that chapter V is the central chapter of the *Two Treatises*. This last point only becomes important if one places a certain emphasis on the statement in Locke's preface to the *Two Treatises* that the all important middle treatise has been lost.

10. But if God provided only the nearly worthless materials (§43), should not the statement read that God meant for nothing to remain worthless? How can something nearly worthless spoil?

11. §§45–48 are all integral for unraveling Locke's teaching on money. Peculiarly, it seems Locke introduces the concept of money for the first time at least twice: "This is certain, that in the beginning . . . man . . . had agreed, that a little piece of yellow metal . . . should be worth a great piece of flesh" (§37). "And thus came the use of money. . . . " (§47).

12. The other side of this might be that because man in isolation will not seek to enlarge his possessions that acquisition is a communal phenomenon. Such might be the case, but Locke would simply fall back on the proposition that this is a treatise of government, and governments are communal, which is why he concerns himself with those situations in which acquisition can occur.

13. Man increases one hundred fold in quantity and quality (§37, §40).

14. When one reads the scriptural reference, and not Locke's paraphrase, at §38, one wonders whether there was ever an instance in which land was not scarce. For the conflict between Abraham and Lot and Esau and Mount Seir was over land, even though Locke denies that it was.

15. At §43 he writes, "nature and the earth furnished only the almost worthless materials," and at §40 he says, "that what in them is purely owing to *nature,* and what to *labour,* we shall find, that in most of them ninety-nine hundredths are wholly to be put on the account of *labour.*"

16. "[P]roperty is to Locke both a natural and a legal right. And it does not seem unfair to say that at times the latter is more important to Locke than the former" (Cherno 1957, p. 51).

17. "Though the earth, and all inferior creatures, be common to all men, yet every man has property in his own person: this nobody has a right to but himself" (§27).

18. At some level, it seems impossible to separate man from property as it is man who created property. The idea of property originates within man when man mixes his labor with what lay in common. Therefore, to deprive man of his property is to deprive man of his labor's fruits, and thus himself.

19. "I answer, each transgression may be punished to that degree [death], and with so much severity, as will suffice to make it an ill bargain to the offender, give him cause to repent, and terrify others from doing the like" (§12). "This makes it lawful for a man to kill a thief, who has not in the least hurt him . . . because using force, where he has no right, to get me into his power, let his pretence be what it will, I have no reason to suppose, that he, who would take away my liberty, would not, when he had me in his power, take away every thing else" (§18). It is also defensible to say that inequality is natural and therefore justified in being protected by government (§6,§34, §54).

20. It will be shown in a later chapter how precisely Madison's thought reflects this understanding of property. But for now, it is enough to say that Madison argues that we have rights in property and property in rights.

21. I thank Michael Zuckert for making this recommendation.

22. The following sections are a few others that make the argument that the end of government is the protection of property: §3, §§87–88, §§94–95, §§123–124, §127, §131, §§134–135, §139, §222.

23. "From the first chapter of the *Second Treatise* to the last, Locke is consistent in stating that political power is instituted primarily for the purpose of protecting or 'preserving' property" (Cherno 1957, p. 53).

24. In fact, a government that takes arbitrary action against property is despotic. "Political, where men have property in their own disposal; and despotical, over such as have no property at all" (§174).

25. This step requires some familiarity with Locke's teaching on slavery. To be taken over by a power that prohibits your freedom, or compels one to do what they otherwise would not, without one's consent is slavery (§17). Moreover, a state of slavery—which is a continued state of war—is a condition in which a man is deprived of his freedom which is his only protection against such arbitrary power (§17, §23). "These men having, as I say, forfeited their lives, and with it their liberties, and lost their estates; and being in the state of slavery, not capable of any property, cannot in that state be considered as any part of civil society; the chief end whereof is the preservation of property" (§85).

26. Even governments must respect this principle, as there is no difference between a government and an individual who threatens man's property. "The supreme power cannot take from any man any part of his property without his own consent: for the preservation of property being the end of government, and that for which men enter into society. . . . Hence it is a mistake to think, that the supreme or legislative power of any common-wealth, can do what it will, and dispose of the estates of the subject arbitrarily, or take any part of them at pleasure" (§138).

Chapter 3

Pre-Constitution America

Prior to the ratification of the U.S. Constitution, there was a long tradition of constitution and compact making that preceded the document drawn up in Philadelphia in 1787. The delegates who came to Philadelphia were not new to politics. While Madison is the most famous example, many of the delegates who met in Philadelphia were active in writing their own state constitutions and all were involved in their state's politics at some level. The common law provides a legal justification for property rights, Locke provides a philosophical justification, and this chapter provides a historical justification for the protection of property rights in modern times. All three areas work together, as the authors of the state constitutions explicitly rely on their common law heritage and Locke—though not explicitly—for their justification of property rights and to explicate the link between property and liberty.

In terms of property rights, most of what the delegates knew came from the Magna Carta and the English common law:

> Guarantees contained in Chapter 29 of the 1225 Magna Carta appeared early in the laws of the colonies, in statutes passed by: Maryland General Assembly in 1639; the Massachusetts Body of Liberties in 1641; the West New Jersey Charter of Fundamental Laws in 1676; and the New York Charter of Liberties and Privileges in 1683. (Siegan 2001, p. 50)

The members of the First Continental Congress in 1774 understood property rights according to their expression in the English constitution and their origin in the law of nature: "The early constitutions of the original states contained provisions with language—comparable to that found in Chapter 29 of the 1225 Magna Carta and in the Declaration of Independence—protecting life, liberty, and property" (Siegan 2001, p. 52).

Because the delegates did not come to the convention void of knowledge and experience, we should not come to their Constitution in any different condition:

> At the time the U.S. Constitution was framed in September, 1787, the Northwest Ordinance and the constitutions of nine of the thirteen state contained Magna Carta–oriented language. . . . The Northwest Ordinance, as well as Vermont's and Massachusetts's constitutions included takings clauses requiring compensation when government deprived owners of their land for public use . . . the state constitutions and common law served as the principal, and sometimes inadequate, barriers to governmental oppressions. It [U.S. Constitution] did not have the power to deprive people of the liberties to which they were entitled by virtue of the common and statutory laws of England and the state in which they lived. (Siegan 2001, p. 67)

Bernard Siegan is not the only legal historian to understand this point. James W. Ely, Jr. has also found that "Throughout the revolutionary era, Americans emphasized the centrality of the right to property in constitutional thought. . . . Hence, the protection of property ownership was an integral part of the American effort to fashion constitutional limits on governmental authority" (Ely 1998, p. 26). And one manner in which property was protected from government seizure in the American founding documents and English common law was by granting compensation for seized property. "The granting of compensation was well established and extensively practiced at and before the time of the Revolution" (Ely 1998, 24).

Chapter 1 argued that property rights are found in English common law. This chapter shows that Americans understood their property rights in the same way their English predecessors did. Through an examination of governing documents from the original states and the Northwest Ordinance, this chapter demonstrates that the protection of property rights was as strong in America as it was in England, and the new nation's understanding of these rights is based in the common law and Lockean understanding of property rights. In examining these documents, the book will show that there is no ideological distinction between property rights and due process rights as there is in modern times. The argument made in this book applies equally to the separation between procedural and substantive due process rights that occurred after the New Deal. But to narrow the scope of inquiry, this chapter focuses primarily on the ideological distinction between procedural due process rights and property rights. The revolutionary era and founding generations valued procedural due process rights for their ability to protect life, liberty, and property. The modern ideological disjunction between due process rights and property rights is the result of political battles played out in the political arena and is not found in the historical foundation or philosophical justification of these rights.

CONNECTICUT

Connecticut, like Rhode Island, did not frame a new constitution in response to the May 1776 congressional recommendation that the new independent state governments do so. Connecticut merely extended its colonial charter as the fundamental law of the state and added three guarantees—stated in four points—that form a brief Declaration of Rights. The second, as it is a forerunner of the Privileges and Immunities Clause of Article IV of the U.S. Constitution and Fifth Amendment of the same document, is what this discussion will focus on. In section 2, the people of Connecticut thought it proper to include property rights and due process rights in the same category:

> That no Man's Life shall be taken away. . . . No Man's Person shall be arrested, restrained, banished, dismembered, nor any Ways Punished. . . . No Man's Goods or estate shall be taken away from him . . . unless clearly warranted by the Laws of this State. (Connecticut Declaration of Rights, 1776, Section 2, p. 290)[1]

While the colonial charters provided a government structure and rules to govern everyday interactions, Connecticut—like eight other states—felt it was necessary to provide a declaration of rights. This is quite consistent with the spirit of the Declaration of Independence. Many of the state's declaration of rights provided protections against the abuses listed in the Declaration of Independence. Prior to 1776, the colonies thought the common law and their colonial charters were clear enough statements of what the government should do and what rights the people retained, but they found out they were wrong and that an explicit statement of those rights that protected the people from the government should be attached to their governing documents. Surely, no one thought paper barriers were sufficient, only that they were necessary.

DELAWARE

Acting through a convention that met on August 17, 1776, Delaware adopted a Declaration of Rights along with its constitution. The Declaration of Rights was adopted on September 11 and the Constitution on September 20 of the same year. Although Maryland's Declaration of Rights was not formerly adopted until two months after Delaware's adoption, Delaware had on hand a draft of it, and there are obvious similarities between the declarations of the two states as well as those of Virginia and Pennsylvania. In all four states, guarantees were made for the protection of life, liberty, property, trial by jury, the right to be informed of an accusation, legal counsel, speedy trial, protections against self-incrimination, excessive bail and fines, and warrantless searches. Delaware was the first state to adopt a provision against quartering soldiers, and section 11 of the Declaration provided the precursor to the U.S. Constitution's prohibition of ex post facto laws. Delaware firmly entrenches itself in the American and common law tradition of the protection of property rights from government seizure and places property—philosophically and rhetorically—alongside life and liberty.

> That every member of society hath a right to be protected in the enjoyment of life, liberty, and property, and therefore is bound to contribute his proportion towards the expense of that protection, and yield his personal service when necessary, or an equivalent thereto; but no part of a man's property can be justly taken from him or applied to public uses without his own consent or that of his legal Representatives: Nor can any man who is conscientiously scrupulous of bearing arms in any case be justly compelled thereto if he will pay such equivalent (Delaware Declaration of Rights, 1776, Section 10, p. 277).
>
> That all warrants without oath to search suspected places, or to seize any person or his property, are grievous and oppressive; and all general warrant to search suspected places . . . without naming or describing the place or any person in special, are illegal and ought not to be granted. (Delaware Declaration of Rights, 1776, Section 17, p. 278)

Delaware recognized the need for a government to use private property for public purposes and the necessity of raising revenue, but each must be done with respect to the law and with the consent of the individual or legal representative. *Legal representative* is a vague phrase that is used in other state declarations. The term is vague because there is no clear indication if this means someone filling the role of legal executor or representative in the legislature. But if we are to read the phrase literally and in context with all other references to representatives throughout the declaration and constitution, it cannot mean political representative. In all other references in Delaware's constitution and declaration to elected or appointed political representatives, they are categorized as such. At no other point is legal representative used synonymously with political representative and therefore cannot be assumed to here. Therefore, the consent must come from the individual or from someone who has the legal authorization to execute his or her wishes.

Also, Delaware shows an understanding of property consistent with Locke in that a person's property and person are equally valuable, and that the value of due process rights, such as those stipulated in section 17, are found in their ability to protect the person and his property. Such an understanding of property rights, and their relationship to other rights, is consistent with what is seen in Locke, other founding documents, and the writings of James Madison.

GEORGIA AND RHODE ISLAND

This may first appear to be an odd pairing, but they are the only two states not to mention property in either a declaration of rights or constitution prior to 1789. These states are obviously an aberration and cannot be said to accurately represent the importance of property rights in pre-Constitution America. However, it needs to be shown that there was some variation among states about the value and importance of property prior to the ratification of the Constitution.

Georgia is unique in its silence on property rights given that it is the only state to ratify a revolutionary era constitution and not mention property rights. Georgia did mention other rights; it did not add anything new as all those mentioned had already been raised in earlier state constitutions. Its silence on property rights must go unexplained for now, though I cannot say for sure if Georgia found them unimportant. And if it did, it obviously did not influence anyone outside of its own borders.

In the case of Rhode Island, no historian would be shocked to find this to be the case. The Charter of Rhode Island and Providence Plantations of 1663 reflected the experience and character of its founder, Roger Williams. Williams left Massachusetts due to religious conflict between himself and the colonists and founded a colony in which religious freedom was the foundational agreement. Even Jews and Quakers were permitted to practice in Rhode Island. Also, Rhode Island did not ratify a new constitution until 1842. Thus, the sentiments that swept through the other colonies were not reflected in Rhode Island's constitutional heritage. Therefore, what can be said of the other colonies in terms of property rights cannot be repeated in the case of Rhode Island. Though, in the next chapter, it will be shown just how important property rights were to the people of Rhode Island because after the ratification of the U.S. Constitution, Rhode Island was one of the states that demanded a Bill of Rights that included property right protections.

MARYLAND

Maryland's Declaration of Rights preceded the body of the constitution; the forty-two articles in the declaration make it the longest early state declaration. Maryland's constitution was unique in its length but also in its language. In the Declaration of Rights, Maryland did not set down strict mandates, but rather set up principles that ought to exist. The principles Maryland found valuable were found in other state constitutions as well. In fact, most of Maryland's constitution is reflected in Pennsylvania's constitution. Maryland relied heavily on its English heritage to establish legal rights and to provide a sense of legitimacy for its current project. The language and the respect for its English heritage was carried over from its pre-revolutionary constitution to its 1776 constitution:

> Be it enacted . . . that all the Inhabitants of this Province being Christians (slaves excepted) Shall have and enjoy all such liberties and immunities priviledges and free customs within this Province as any naturall born subject of England hath or ought to have or enjoy in the Realm of England . . . by vertue of the common law . . . And shall not be imprisoned nor disseissed or dispossessed of their freehold goods or Chattles or be out Lawed Exiled or otherwise destroyed fore judged or punished then according to the Laws. . . . (Maryland Act for the Liberties of the People, 1639, p. 68)

The 1639 Constitution of Maryland left no doubt that the people of Maryland enjoyed the rights of Englishmen, which included due process protections.

The language and guarantees granted by the 1639 Constitution were reflected in the 1776 version:

> That the trial of facts where they arise, is one of the greatest securities of the lives, liberties, and estates of the people. (Maryland Declaration of Rights, 1776, Section 18, p. 281)
>
> That no freeman ought to be taken, or imprisoned, or disseized of his freehold, liberties, or privileges . . . or deprived of his life, liberty, or property, but by the judgment of his peers, or by the law of the land. (Maryland Declaration of Rights, 1776, Section 21, p. 282)

The similarities between the 1639 document and the 1776 document are undeniable. The rights the people of Maryland thought valuable did not change; they only thought that England no longer protected those rights. The rights of Englishmen were common law rights developed originally in the Magna Carta. The people of Maryland, like other revolutionary colonies, saw no reason to reinvent the wheel. There were rights they thought important and found them in their English legal tradition, such as due process rights and property rights. "That the inhabitants of Maryland are entitled to the common law of England . . . and the inhabitants of Maryland are also entitled to all property derived to them from or under the charter. . . ." (Maryland Declaration of Rights, 1776, Section 3, p. 280).

There was some amount of diversity among the settlers in Maryland, but even those settlers without English ties held similar values. As a group of German settlers in Maryland proclaimed in 1763, "The law of the land is so constituted, that every man is secure in the enjoyment of his property, the meanest person is out of reach of oppression from the most powerful, nor can anything be taken from him without his receiving satisfaction for it" (Ely 1998, p. 16). There is no denying Maryland's commitment to property in its constitutions or its people.

MASSACHUSETTS

Like Maryland, Massachusetts has a lengthy Declaration of Rights that preceded its constitution. These rights were written in precise language so as to leave no question about their intent. Also, like Maryland, Massachusetts had a rich constitutional history whose values were reflected in its 1780 iteration. In 1641, still under British rule, the people of Massachusetts drafted a body of liberties that provided common law rights to its citizens:

No mans life shall be taken away, no mans honour or good name shall be strayned, no mans person shall be arrested, restrained, banished, dismembered, nor any wayes punished, no man shall be deprived of his wife or children, no mans goods or estaite shall be taken away from him, nor any way indammaged . . . unlesse it be by vertue or equitie of some expresse law of the Country. . . . (Massachusetts Body of Liberties, 1641, Section 1, p. 72)

No mans Cattel or goods of what kinde soever shall be pressed or taken form any publique use or service, unlesse it be by warrant grounded upon some act of the generall Court, nor without reasonable prices and hire as the ordinaire rates of the Countrie do afford. (Massachusetts Body of Liberties, 1641, Section 8, p. 73)

The importance Massachusetts placed on property is undeniable. Whether it was land, possessions, or liberty, property was to be protected by the government:

The importance of property—and rights in general—was transferred from 1641 to 1780.

The end of the institution, maintenance, and administration of government, is to secure the existence of the body-politic; to protect it; and to furnish the individuals who compose it, with the power of enjoying, in safety and tranquility, their natural rights, and the blessings of life; And whenever these great objects are not obtained, the people have a right to alter the government, and to take measures necessary for their safety, prosperity, and happiness. (Massachusetts Declaration of Rights, 1780, Preamble, p. 339)

Each individual of the society has a right to be protected by it in the enjoyment of his life, liberty, and property, according to standing laws. . . . But no part of the property of the individual, can, with justice, be taken from him, or applied to public uses without his own consent, or that of the representative body of the people. . . . And whenever the public exigencies require, that the property of any individual should be appropriated to public uses, he shall receive a reasonable compensation therefore. (Massachusetts Declaration of Rights, 1780, Section 10, p. 341–342)

The language is indisputable and leaves nothing to doubt. It is also noteworthy that Massachusetts, one of the most influential colonies and early states, found it necessary to provide a compensation provision when the government found it necessary to seize private property.

NEW HAMPSHIRE

New Hampshire was one of the first states to draft a new constitution in 1776. Its first constitution did not have a declaration of rights. In 1778 and 1781, the state met to ratify a new constitution, both times rejected. In October 1783, the state drafted and passed a new constitution accompanied by a bill of rights. The New Hampshire Bill of Rights provided the same protections and prohibitions as the state documents in Massachusetts, Maryland, Virginia, Pennsylvania, and Delaware. Of course, there were some differences, such as there is no bill of attainder provision in the New Hampshire Bill of Rights, but each state provided protections for intrinsic and instrumental rights. New Hampshire also made its own additions not included by the other states. New Hampshire provided the most stringent separation between church and state and included a double-jeopardy provision. In any event, New Hampshire provided explicit protections of private property:

All men have certain natural, essential, and inherent rights; among which are—the enjoying and defending life and liberty—acquiring, possessing, and protecting property—and in a word, of seeking and obtaining happiness. (New Hampshire Bill of Rights, 1783, Section II, p. 375)

When men enter into a state of society, they surrender up some of their natural rights to that society, in order to insure the protection of others; and, without such an equivalent, the surrender is void. (New Hampshire Bill of Rights, 1783, Section III, p. 375)

Every member of the community has a right to be protected by it in the enjoyment of life, liberty, and property. . . . But no part of a man's property shall be taken from him, or applied to public uses, without his own consent, or that of the representative body of the people. (New Hampshire Bill of Rights, 1783, Section XII, p. 376)

It is essential to the preservation of the rights of every individual, his life, liberty, property, and character, that there be an impartial interpretation of the laws and administration of justice. (New Hampshire Bill of Rights, 1783, Section XXXV, p. 379)

The New Hampshire Bill of Rights reflects a Lockean theory of property.

The supreme power cannot take away from any man any part of his property without his own consent: for the preservation of property being the end of government, and that for which men enter into society, it necessarily supposes and requires, that the people should have property, without which they must be supposed to lose that, by entering into society, which was the end for which they entered into it; too gross an absurdity for any man to own. (§138)

Property, and the possession and acquisition thereof, is synonymous with happiness, and property must be protected by the government. In forming a government the people turn some of their rights over to the government in exchange for more stability and enjoyment in the rights they retain. It is only under the rule of law that man may enjoy his property. But, at no time can the government act against a man's property without his consent or that of his representative.

While the New Hampshire convention does not address the dissolution of government, we may safely assume that when the government does not protect property, given its role in the signing of Declaration of Independence and in the Revolutionary War, that it also supports Locke's recommendation in chapter XIX of the *Second Treatise*.

NEW JERSEY

The New Jersey Constitution of 1776 did not have a separate declaration of rights, but certain articles, particularly XVI–XIX and XXII, served the same purpose. The liberties discussed in the articles all used mandatory formulations and were consistent with other colonial constitutions. Given the structure and brevity of the New Jersey constitution, it is difficult to say for certain which rights they felt were most fundamental to the welfare of a state. If they did make an attempt to codify only those rights they found most valuable, then instrumental rights were among those they found most valuable:

> That the common law of England, as well as so much of the statute law, as have been heretofore practiced in this Colony, shall still remain in force, until they shall be altered by a future law of the Legislature; such parts only excerpted, as are repugnant to the rights and privileges contained in this Charter; and that inestimable right of trial by jury shall remain confirmed as a part of the law of this Colony, without repeal, forever. (New Jersey Constitution, 1776, Section 22, p. 260)

But it is not stipulated to what ends these instrumental rights are to be preserved. It would be safe to assume that the ends of life, liberty, and property are what they had in mind given the constitution's reliance on the common law of England and the property requirements one had to meet in order to hold public office. Moreover, perhaps provisions of property were not included as the assumption was that since those in office would have substantial property holdings, there would be no threat of the passage of laws that would threaten property rights.

But to get a complete sense of what the people of New Jersey thought of property as it related to their legal tradition, one of the earlier constitutions should be cited:

> That no Proprietor, freeholder, or inhabitant of the said Province of West New Jersey, shall be deprived . . . of life, limb, liberty, estate, property . . . without a due trial, and judgment passed by twelve good and lawful men of his neighborhood. . . . (Concessions and Agreements of West New Jersey, 1677, chapter 17, p. 127)

We see the same commitment to instrumental rights as we do in the Constitution of 1776, but this time the ends of those instrumental rights are stated. And because the 1776 constitution acknowledged the authority of the common law and statute law that did not violate the Constitution of 1776, we can now safely reach the conclusion that the value of instrumental rights is their ability to protect life, liberty, and property.

NEW YORK

Of the rights codified in the federal Bill of Rights, many are drawn from guarantees contained in the enactments of the colonists prior to the Constitution's ratification. Massachusetts is the most cited example to this point, but the New York Charter of Libertyes and Priviledges of 1683 supplies many of the same provisions. This document was written as a direct result of a struggle for self-government, precisely the same instance in which the men in Philadelphia found themselves. Many of the provisions were drawn from the Magna Carta, specifically chapter 39 of 1215. "That Noe freeman shall be taken or imprisoned . . . But by the Lawfull Judgment of his peers and by the Law of his province" (New York Charter of Libertyes and Priviledges, 1683, p. 165).

But, again the question arises, to what end are these instrumental rights useful? The answer seems to be similar to what other colonies considered useful:

> That Noe man of what Estate or Condicon soever shall be putt out of his Lands or Tenements, nor taken, nor imprisoned, nor disherited, nor banished nor any wayes destroyed without being brought to Answere by due Course of Law. (New York Charter of Libertyes and Priviledges, 1683, p. 165)
>
> That from hence forward Noe Lands Within this province shall be Esteemed or accounted a Chattle or personall Estate . . . according to the Custome and practice of his Majesties Realme of England." (New York Charter of Libertyes and Priviledges, 1683, p. 166)

New York, much like the other colonies, granted themselves the rights of Englishmen, specifically those rights found at common law.

New York's constitutional tradition continued to reflect these same values in later iterations. New York's Constitution of 1777 reiterated what its citizens had always understood to be their fundamental rights. Oddly, New York did not contain a declaration of rights. This is particularly odd when one considers how vocal the state was in demanding the federal adoption of a Bill of Rights. Even so, Article XXXV recognized common law protections and liberties, including property rights that could only be taken through due process as defined at common law.

NORTH CAROLINA

On November 13, 1776, North Carolina delegates selected a committee to prepare a Declaration of Rights and Constitution. In terms of property rights, the committee decided

> That no freeman ought to be taken, imprisoned, or disseized of his freehold, liberties, or privileges, or outlawed, or exiled, or in any manner destroyed, or deprived of his life, liberty, or property, but by the law of the land. (North Carolina Declaration of Rights, 1776, XII, p. 287)

That in all controversies at law, respecting property, the ancient model of trial, by jury, is one of the best securities of the rights of the people, and ought to remain never to be restrained. (North Carolina Declaration of Rights, 1776, p. 287)

The property of the soil, in a free government, being one of the essential rights of the collective body of the people, it is necessary, in order to avoid future disputes, that the limits of the state should be ascertained with precision. . . . (North Carolina Declaration of Rights, 1776, p. 288)

By referring to property of the soil as being one of the essential rights, and then giving the people the ability to protect that right from government and private infringement, North Carolina put the importance of property alongside the protection of life, liberty, and similar intrinsic rights.

While most of the North Carolina document is replicated in the documents of Virginia, Pennsylvania, Delaware, and Maryland, North Carolina did make a powerful statement about the value of rights and liberties. States like North Carolina—that is, states that did not add much to the dialogue by way of originality—confirm the outlook that prior to the ratification of the U.S. Constitution and the Bill of Rights, there was already a tradition established in America that government should protect an individual's right to property, and it is the responsibility of the people to make sure that the government does not infringe on the very right government was instituted to protect.

PENNSYLVANIA

Given the prominence of William Penn—someone of immense wealth—during the writing of the Pennsylvania Charter of Privileges, 1701, it is no surprise that property is given such a high priority. To preserve property, Penn and the delegates in Pennsylvania turned to a source in which they were familiar—the Magna Carta and English common law:

That no Person or Persons shall or may, at any Time hereafter, be obliged to answer any Complaint, Matter or Thing whatsoever, relating to Property, before the Governor and Council, or in any other Place, but in ordinary Course of Justice, unless Appeals thereunto shall be hereafter by Law appointed. (Pennsylvania Charter of Privileges, 1701, Section 6, p. 173)

In no other section is property mentioned, thus giving us certainty that the only means by which someone could be deprived of his or her property was through the proper legal channels. There was no provision for taking someone's property for the common good, even with compensation. The only people who could be deprived of property were criminals or those in debt to another private citizen.

In 1776, Pennsylvania replaced the Pennsylvania Charter of Privileges with a new constitution and Declaration of Rights. This constitution was substantially longer than the previous one, and thus the provisions protecting property, and thus liberty, were much more extensive. The Declaration of Rights begins by stating the fundamental characteristics of man and his rights:

> That all men are born equally free and independent, and have certain natural, inherent, and inalienable rights, amongst which are, the enjoying and defending life and liberty, acquiring, possessing, and protecting property, and pursuing and obtaining happiness and safety. (Pennsylvania Declaration of Rights, 1776, Section 1, p. 264)

This sentiment is expressed in a later section that adds a more explicit statement about what rights government ought to protect:

> That every member of society hath a right to be protected in the enjoyment of life, liberty, and property, and therefore is bound to contribute his proportion towards the expence of that protection, and yield his personal service when necessary, or an equivalent thereto: But no part of a man's property can be justly taken from him, or applied to public uses, without his own consent, or that of his legal representatives: Nor can any man who is conscientiously scrupulous of bearing arms, be justly compelled thereto, if he will pay such equivalent, nor are the people bound by any laws, but such as they have in like manner assented to, for their common good. (Pennsylvania Declaration of Rights, 1776, Section 8, p. 265)

While real property was protected from seizures in section 8, which would have been enough for some colonies, Pennsylvania extended this right that would later be included in the Fifth and Fourteenth Amendments:

> That the people have a right to hold themselves, their houses, papers, and possessions free from search and seizure, and therefore warrants without oaths or affirmations first made, affording a sufficient foundation for them, and whereby any officer or messenger may be commanded or required to search suspected places, or to seize any person or persons, his or their property, not particularly described, are contrary to that right, and ought not to be granted. (Pennsylvania Declaration of Rights, 1776, Section 10, p. 265)
> That in controversies respecting property, and in suits between man and man, the parties have a right to trial by jury, which ought to be held sacred. (Pennsylvania Declaration of Rights, 1776, Section 11, p. 265).

Pennsylvania expresses clearly the link between property and liberty as well as the connection between instrumental rights and property rights.

Property rights could only be protected through instrumental rights grounded in the common law. Moreover, landed property was considered along the same dimension as other types of rights just as is seen in the Fifth Amendment of the federal Bill of Rights.

These points, while not broadly discussed, have been recognized by some of the more careful legal scholars. Robert Palmer writes, "The subject matter of the Pennsylvania declaration of rights is republican. Many of its provisions protect individual liberties: rights to life, liberty, property" (Palmer 1987, p. 62). Palmer continues in his essay to show that many of the colonial constitutions, particularly Pennsylvania, served as models for the federal Bill of Rights.

SOUTH CAROLINA

While it does not have a distinct declaration of rights, many of the rights given in the body of the South Carolina Constitution are reflected in the New York and Massachusetts constitutions. South Carolina does not add anything new to our understanding of the post-1776 period; it merely reinforces what has already been said: property rights are a necessary condition for the preservation of liberty, as property and liberty are inseparable:

> That no freeman of this State be taken or imprisoned, or disseized of his freehold, liberties, or privileges, or outlawed, exiled, or in any manner destroyed or deprived of his life, liberty, or property, but by the judgment of his peers or by the law of the land. (South Carolina Constitution, 1778, Section 41, p. 335)

While unstated in New Jersey's constitution, the obvious ends for instrumental rights in South Carolina is the preservation of property and its related components. This explication of the ends of instrumental rights is more explicit here than it was in the New Jersey documents.

VERMONT

The Vermont Constitution of 1777 was the first by a state that had not been a separate colony before independence. Though Vermont did not become a state until 1791, it set up its own government in 1777. Because this is the case, Vermont can only be used as a barometer for the general feeling on property rights that existed in New England rather than a state that had a direct influence on the constitutional understanding of property rights because it did not send any delegates to the Philadelphia Convention or first Congress.

There can be no doubt of Vermont's position on the principles embodied in the Declaration of Independence or those rights protected by the U.S. Constitution and Bill of Rights. In its first chapter, the Vermont Declaration of Rights states, "That all men are born equally free and independent, and have certain natural, inherent, and unalienable rights, amongst which are the enjoying and defending of life and liberty; acquiring, possessing, and protecting property, and pursuing and obtaining happiness and safety. . . ." (Vermont Declaration of Rights, 1777, chapter 1.1, p. 322). Vermont's was one of the earliest constitutions, but it copied nearly every word of the Pennsylvania Constitution, and its Declaration of Rights provided the same intrinsic and instrumental rights that the Pennsylvania Declaration of Rights provided. Vermont, unlike Pennsylvania, did provide a provision in its constitution that outlaws slavery and indentured servitude. This provision speaks directly to the value placed on liberty and equality by the people of Vermont.

Vermont's protection of all liberties, and its progressive view of equality, gives credibility to the protection they give to property rights. One might accuse current property rights advocates of being caught up in an arcane system of rights and laws that reflects an elitist mentality. Vermont serves as a counterexample to this claim, one which helps set the stage for the final two chapters of this book, which provide empirical evidence to refute such criticisms.

Like its commitment to other rights, Vermont's position on property is written with such clarity that there can be no doubt in the reader's mind that property must be protected by government in order to ensure liberty. Vermont was also pragmatic in its valuation of property rights:

> That private property ought to be subservient to public uses, when necessity requires it; nevertheless, whenever any particular man's property is taken for the use of the public, the owner ought to receive an equivalent in money (Vermont Declaration of Rights, 1777, chapter 1.2, p. 322). . . . That government is, or ought to be, instituted for the common benefit, protection, and security of the people . . . not for the particular emolument or advantage of any single man, family, or set of men. . . . (Vermont Declaration of Rights, 1777, chapter 1.5, p. 323)

Vermont's commitment to property rights was intertwined with other rights, which reflects the common law understanding of rights:

> That the people have a right to hold themselves, their houses, papers, and possessions free from search or seizure; and therefore warrants, without oaths or affirmations first made, affording a sufficient foundation for them, and whereby any officer or messenger may be commanded or required to search suspected

places, or to seize any persons or persons, his, her, or their property, nor
particularly described, are contrary to that rights, and ought not to be granted.
(Vermont Declaration of Rights, 1777, chapter 1.11, p. 323)

That Vermont's treatment of rights is so comprehensive, it makes Vermont
an important component to the study of American rights prior to the ratification
of the Constitution. Vermont displays a commitment to rights grounded in the
common law tradition that was inherited by the other colonies.

VIRGINIA

Virginia is an important state in the development of the federal Bill of Rights
because of the role James Madison played in drafting and ratifying the federal
Constitution and Bill of Rights. Madison joined the Virginia constitutional
committee on May 16 and immediately took an active role in the constitution's development. Perhaps because of his youth, he did not play as large a
part in the Virginia constitutional committee as he would at the Philadelphia
Constitutional Convention, but he was active nonetheless. What is expressed
in the Virginia Declaration of Rights anticipates Madison's concerns, which
he would express in the first Congress. Moreover, the Virginia Declaration of
Rights of 1776 helped serve as a template—along with other state constitutions—for the federal Bill of Rights.

Like Massachusetts, Pennsylvania, New York and others, there is a clear
connection between liberty and property in the Virginia Declaration of
Rights:

> That all men are by nature equally free and independent, and have certain
> inherent rights, of which, when they enter into a state of society, they cannot,
> by any compact, deprive, or divest their posterity; namely, the enjoyment of life
> and liberty, with the means of acquiring and possessing property, and persu-
> ing and obtaining happiness and safety. (Virginia Declaration of Rights, 1776,
> Section 1, p. 234)
> [A]ll men . . . have the right to suffrage, and cannot be taxed or deprived of
> their property for publick uses without their own consent or that of their Rep-
> resentative so elected, nor bound by any law to which they have not, in like
> manner, assented, for the publick good. (Virginia Declaration of Rights, 1776,
> Section 6, p. 234)

Also, those instrumental rights that are thought valuable by the federal
Bill of Rights in the protection of property rights are also thought valuable
in 1776 Virginia:

That in controversies respecting property, and in suits between man and man, the ancient trial by Jury is preferable to any other, and ought to be held sacred. (Virginia Declaration of Rights, 1776, Section 11, p. 235)

Palmer writes, "Virginia adopted its Declaration of Rights before and separate from its constitution. The Virginia Declaration of Rights, like Pennsylvania's, contained provisions important to communal rights as well as individual liberties" (Palmer 1987, p. 67). What Palmer neglects to mention is the importance placed on individual liberties by the Virginia constitutional committee. It is clearly seen through a reading of the document that individual liberties are what allow communal rights to exist. Without individual liberties, communal rights could be transformed into communal domination of the individual.

NORTHWEST ORDINANCE

If a nation were able to set up a system of law that would govern a new territory so as not to reflect the demands of local politics, the system might look differently than other constitutions and perhaps reflect ideals more accurately. This assumption is what drives this examination of the Northwest Ordinance. There were certainly political battles played out while drafting the Ordinance, particularly over the slavery issue. But when drafting the Ordinance, the drafters did not have to court local constituencies or be concerned with anything but what would be in the best interest of that region. That being the case, the Northwest Ordinance's protection and espousal of property rights is perhaps the best reflection of the nation's position on the question prior to the ratification of the Bill of Rights. Like Vermont, the Northwest Ordinance was progressive. All the rights granted to the settlers were granted to Indians in the territory as well. This is quite a remarkable departure from the treatment of Indians in the colonies.

The Northwest Ordinance spoke in general terms and mixed property rights with other rights. This continues the trend seen in the state constitutions and declaration of rights. However, it should be noted that property could only be taken for preservation of the community, which is a greater restriction than saying for the public good. Property could be seized, with compensation and through a jury trial, if the survival of the community required it:

And to secure the rights of personal liberty and property to the inhabitants and others, purchasers in the said territory, it is hereby ordained, that the inhabitants thereof shall always be entitled to the benefits of the act of *habeas corpus,* and of the trial by jury. (Northwest Ordinance, 1787, p. 389)

No man shall be deprived of his liberty or property but by the judgment of
his peers or the law of the land, and should the public exigencies make it necessary for the common preservation to take any persons property or to demand his
particular services, full compensation shall be made therefore. . . . (Northwest
Ordinance, 1787, p. 395)

This brings the total number of documents requiring compensation for
property seizures to three, which is greater than the number previously
thought.[2] It previously had been recorded that there were no states that provided such a provision (Dumbauld 1957, p. 160–165; reprinted in Levy 1999,
p. 264–268). But, as seen above, by simply consulting the documents, this
error in calculation can be avoided.

SUMMARY

This chapter has shown the conditions that must be met to make property seizure legitimate and the methods by which property can be legitimately seized.
Working together, the government's ability to seize property was severely
restricted by these pre-Constitution documents. Property seizure must be done
for the public good in such a manner that also allows for public use of that property. This is a two-pronged test that is sometimes ignored. First, the result of the
property seizure must provide for the public good. This means that the public
must be better off after the property seizure than it was before. This can allow
for a broad reading, but only if the historical context and the second prong of
the test are ignored. In one state that drafted a declaration of rights prior to the
Constitution, the criteria are more stringent by authorizing a seizure only when
the existence of the community is at stake. The second prong of the test requires
that a property, when seized, be made available for public use.

Thus, it is clear what conditions must be met in order to seize property. The
constitutions of the states also address what institutional mechanisms can be
used to seize private property if the previous two-prong test has been passed.
To legitimately take property, three states (Delaware, New Hampshire, and
Pennsylvania) allow seizures only through the individual's consent or the
consent of his representatives. As argued above, representative does not
necessarily mean political representative. To repeat, there is a requirement in
these states that it must be done in accord with the public good and for public
use. There are two states (Connecticut and New York) that authorize seizures
only if the law allows for it. Four states (Maryland, Massachusetts, North
Carolina, and South Carolina) allow for seizures under the law coupled with
some other mechanism such as consent or a jury trial. West New Jersey and

the Northwest Ordinance authorize deprivation of property only through jury trials. Five states (Maryland, North Carolina, Pennsylvania, South Carolina, and Virginia) authorize seizures through jury trials coupled with either consent or legal authorization. Some states do not provide a method by which property can be seized but rather rely on the rules of common law to resolve disputes, which then implicates jury trials. In each instance, there are strict guidelines in place to protect the people from illegitimate property seizures.

These documents also tell us why property rights are important so that we may understand their stature within the Fifth Amendment. And like the earlier documents, more than just the protection of property rights, the Fifth Amendment provides protection of other right:

> No person shall be held to answer for a capital, or otherwise infamous crime, unless on a presentment or indictment of a grand jury, except in cases arising in the land of naval forces, or in the militia, when in actual service in time of war or public danger; nor shall any person be subject for the same offense to be twice put in jeopardy of life or limb; nor shall be compelled in any criminal cases to be a witness against himself, nor be deprived of life, liberty, or property, without due process of law; nor shall private property be taken for public use, without just compensation.

What at first seems like an odd collection of rights begins to make sense when the intellectual and historical heritage of the Fifth Amendment is considered. First, of the founding documents discussed above that specifically mention property rights, they all do so in the same style the Fifth Amendment does. That is, the authors of the Fifth Amendment simply adopted the rhetorical style of those who came before them, and in some cases, the men who drew up the state constitutions also played a role in the ratification of the Fifth Amendment. Second, the procedural rights outlined in the Fifth Amendment are drawn from the state constitutions that preceded it. The state constitutions recognized that procedural rights were not an end, but a means for protecting life, liberty, and property. Also, as Locke argues, and as the state constitutions treat the topic—as well as the Northwest Ordinance—liberty and property are inseparable, and life is unbearable without either. The collection of rights in the Fifth Amendment reflect this understanding. The procedural rights are drawn from the common law, and they are in place for the protection of property, just as they were at common law. From a historical perspective, we are left to conclude that property must be protected through the procedural rights outlined in the Fifth Amendment; in fact, that is their primary intention because to protect property is to protect liberty and all other rights that spring from those.

Willi Paul Adams, in his seminal study on early state constitutions, sees things a bit differently, however. Adams argues that the attachment to property by the colonists was beginning to fade even before 1776, much less by the time the ratification of the Constitution was put to the states (Adams 1980, p. 160). This is probably due to the fact that Adams considers property only in terms of physical property, or commerce, and not in its dual sense (Adams 1980, p. 161). He cites as evidence, seemingly his only evidence, the substitution of "pursuit of happiness" for "property" in the Declaration of Independence by Thomas Jefferson. There are a number of reasons this could have occurred that would challenge Adams's thesis. But the one I find most convincing is that property and the pursuit of happiness were interchangeable—not identical—terms. Willi Paul Adams seems to agree with this argument against his own thesis when he writes, "One of the reasons was that the acquisition of property and the pursuit of happiness were so closely connected with each other in the minds of the founding generation that naming only one of the two sufficed to evoke both" (Adams 1980, p. 193). Furthermore, Adams argues earlier in his book that life, liberty, and property were protected by state bills of rights against government and majority infringement as these rights are found in natural law and social contract theory. These rights, he argues, are inalienable rights (Adams 1980, p. 145).

Perhaps what I see as confusion and contradiction in Adams could have been avoided by adopting a unity of rights reading of the documents under consideration. Such a reading would show that there is no conflict between political liberty and property, but rather, one could not exist without the other. This seems to be the case for the Magna Carta, Locke, the revolutionary generation, and the architects of the U.S. Bill of Rights.

To move one, by examining these early documents, legal scholars and jurists should be able to grasp more accurately the relationship between property rights and due process rights as well as the conditions that must be met before property can be seized. Of course, the practice of the law is different from the letter of the law, and surely, property rights were trampled during the war effort against the British and the subsequent rebuilding of the nation. Outrage over these events, I argue, encouraged the framers of the Constitution and the Bill of Rights to adopt stringent protections of property rights in the new documents. That is, they witnessed firsthand that when property is trampled, so too are all the ends of government.

NOTES

1. All references to state documents and the Northwest Ordinance are taken from Schwartz 1971. Page numbers refer to Schwartz 1971.
2. The number grows when one recalls Pennsylvania's refusal to make property seizure legitimate by any means.

Chapter 4

The Constitution's View
of Property

The previous chapter tried to show that the construction of the Fifth Amendment was not an accident, nor was it a political maneuver by James Madison to get the protection of property passed without detection (Amar 1998, p. 78).[1] Drawing on the state constitutions and the Northwest Ordinance, I have shown that the Fifth Amendment reflects the rhetorical style of the state constitutions as well as the values of the framers who considered liberty and property inseparably linked, and that the end of due process (instrumental) rights was the preservation of life, liberty, and property.

We know that in pre-Constitution America there was a high value placed on property, as one commentator wrote, "The right to property is the guardian of every other right, and to deprive a people of this, is in fact to deprive them of liberty" (Lee 1775, p. 14). It is safe to assume that little changed from the revolutionary era to post-Constitution America with regard to the people's disposition toward property if one hundred years later Alexis de Tocqueville could write, "In no other country in the world is the love of property keener or more alert than in the United States, and nowhere else does the majority display less inclination toward doctrines which in any way threaten the way property is owned" (Tocqueville 1969, 638–639). This sentiment in Tocqueville's era was reinforced by such jurists as Joseph Story, who remarked, "Indeed, in a free government, almost all other rights would become worthless if the government possessed an uncontrollable power over the private fortune of every citizen" (Story 1833, Section 1790). But we need not move to Tocqueville or Story for evidence just yet, as influential statesmen in the early republic commonly remarked, "Property must be secured or liberty cannot exist" (Adams 1851, p. 280). No statement puts the point more forcefully than Alexander Hamilton's, who said in the context of property, "a power over a man's subsistence amounts to a power over his will" (#79: p. 408), or, "One great object of government is personal protection and the security of property" (Hamilton 1937, p. 302). Of course, Hamilton and Adams were not alone; John Rutledge said, "Property was certainly the principal object of society" (Rutledge 1980, p. 191).

This chapter centers on those who took part in the ratification of the Bill of Rights, specifically James Madison, who was the architect of the Bill of Rights.[2] In order to properly understand the Court's deviation from the Fifth Amendment in *Kelo*, it is necessary to understand not only how important property rights were to the founding generation, but how they were understood by Madison and those who ratified the Bill of Rights. "The records of the convention reveal that only one delegate disputed the primacy of property rights. For James Wilson 'the cultivation and enforcement of the human mind was the most noble object' of government and society" (Siegan 1997, p. 15). The others at the Philadelphia Convention, and those who crafted and ratified the Bill of Rights, can accurately be positioned alongside Madison, who wrote, "Where an excess of power prevails, property of no sort is duly respected. No man is safe in his opinions, his person, his faculties, or his possessions" (Madison 1999, p. 515).

The next chapter discusses the interpretation the Supreme Court gave to public good in *Kelo*, this chapter demonstrates that when the historical evidence is examined, property protection is the first object of government, and if it is to be compromised for the public good, the link to the government policy and the benefits it bestows upon the public must be real and direct. The balance, in the minds of the founding generation, between public good and private property tipped in favor of private property, as property and liberty are inseparable; and if liberty is compromised, there can be no public good worth having. Liberty vanishes when the government collapses or becomes tyrannical, this we learn from Locke. But what we also learn from Locke, and Madison, is that government violates its intended purpose when it fails to protect property. This chapter does not provide the original definition of public use, but it does provide a rubric we can apply to questions of public use that allows us to know if a particular public use is important enough to overtake the right to property.

I. DEMANDS FROM THE STATES

For those who may not know, when the men in Philadelphia were finished drafting the new Constitution, there was still plenty of work to be done. Nine of the thirteen states had to approve the new document if it were to replace the Articles of Confederation. Some people were skeptical about a document that was drawn up in secret by men who had usurped their duties by drafting a new document. There were also a number of substantive concerns, such as the power of the national government relative to the states under the new document. But one of the most pressing matters was the lack of a Bill of Rights. The states felt that unless specific rights were spelled out in the document, there was a high risk of losing those rights. One of the rights not afforded explicit protection in the original document was property rights, and the thirteen states immediately recognized this omission. When reading the states' reactions to this omission, it is clear that the attachment the people in the states had to property rights was not diminished with the ratification of a new constitution.

On Friday December 12, 1787, in Pennsylvania, the state legislature suggested that the national government add a number of provisions, two of which directly addressed their concern for property: "(2) That in controversies respecting property . . . trial by jury shall remain. . . . (5) That warrants unsupported by evidence, whereby any officer or messenger may seize . . . property . . . shall not be granted. . . ." (Pennsylvania Legislative Records Dec. 12, 1787, p. 658).[3] Just as they demanded it in their own constitution and declaration of rights, the people of Pennsylvania demanded that property be guaranteed in the national governing document and protected through procedural measures also outlined in the same document. That being the case, Pennsylvania still ratified, even without a Bill of Rights.

The fifth state to ratify, Massachusetts, did so without a national Bill of Rights but recommended that one be added. Massachusetts was a key figure in getting a national Bill of Rights adopted as they were the first state to submit their recommended amendments to Congress with their ratification. South Carolina followed Massachusetts's model and sent four proposed amendments to Congress with the ratified Constitution. Maryland, the seventh state to ratify, also offered amendments but did not send them to Congress. Instead, they submitted them in pamphlet form to the people of Maryland in order to gain popular support for the measures. New Hampshire, the ninth state to ratify, and thus bringing the Constitution into effect, could only get the ratification passed in the legislature by adding twelve amendments to the document in order to pacify the Anti-Federalist opposition. While each of these states proposed amendments in one form or another, the recommendations were nonbinding on the federal government, even though James Madison assured the states a Bill of Rights would be added.

With nine states on board, the new country was constitutionally created. But everyone knew that without Virginia and New York, the new nation would fail. All the delegates who drafted the 1776 Virginia Declaration of Rights were also at the 1788 ratification convention, including James Madison. The home state of James Madison, the architect of the national Bill of

Rights, was the first state to have its own Bill of Rights after 1787, and
therefore it is no surprise that this state would want the national Constitution
to have the same:

> Of particular interest to this study are the following amendments proposed by
> Virginia.
>
> 1st That there are certain natural rights, of which men, when they form a
> social compact, cannot deprive or divest their posterity; among which are the
> enjoyment of life and liberty, with the means of acquiring, possessing, and
> protecting property, and pursuing and obtaining happiness and safety. (p. 840)
>
> 9th That no freeman ought to be taken, imprisoned, or disseized of his
> freehold liberties, privileges, or franchises, or outlawed, or exiled, or in any
> manner destroyed, or deprived of his life, liberty, or property, but by the law of
> the land. (p. 841)
>
> 11th That, in controversies respecting property . . . the ancient trial by jury is
> one of the greatest securities. . . . (p. 841)
>
> 12th That every freeman ought to find a certain remedy, by recourse to the
> laws, for all injuries and wrongs he may receive in his person, property, or
> character. (p. 841)
>
> 14th That every freeman has a right to be secure from all unreasonable
> searches and seizures of his person, his papers, and property. . . . (p. 841)

What can be seen in these amendments is a clear commitment to the
preservation of property through those instrumental rights found at common
law and codified in pre-Constitution state constitutions, as well as an understanding of property that makes its preservation necessary for life and liberty.
Property is a natural right which government is created to protect, and without
which, safety and happiness are sacrificed. The laws and legal institutions, as
understood by the legislature of Virginia, are to be designed with the express
purpose of protecting property. Whether by jury trial or law, a person's property was to be protected from both government and private individuals. The
government was designed to settle disputes between individuals; the Constitution and Bill of Rights were designed to make sure that those same laws
applied to the government's interaction with individuals.

Virginia's proposal had a profound influence on other hold-out states as
well. North Carolina's ratification of the Constitution contained identical
language. Rhode Island's ratification, which occurred after the Bill of Rights
had been ratified, differed only on small matters (Siegan 1997, p. 25). While
North Carolina did not vary from Virginia, it is significant in that it signals
how important these rights were to a large segment of the population. Rhode
Island makes no mention of property in its amendments, but makes known
its position—which was identical to Virginia's—by making eighteen declarations of how they read the Constitution and the rights they found valuable.

New York was the home state of Alexander Hamilton. Though Hamilton and Madison, along with Jay, authored the *Federalist Papers,* their thought did diverge on the question of the Bill of Rights. Madison thought it was superfluous, so there was no harm in adding it, especially if it would help move the ratification process along and keep the states satisfied once ratified. Hamilton, on the other hand, understood a Bill of Rights to be dangerous. He suggested that if a Bill of Rights were added, people would think that the list was exclusive, meaning, the only rights the government is designed to protect are those listed. Hamilton thought that, because there were so many rights, some would be overlooked and potentially left unprotected. But Hamilton was fighting a losing battle and acquiesced.

The debate in New York was far more divisive than in Virginia as both sides had equally powerful figures[4] and the sides were further apart than they were in Virginia. The convention assembled on June 27, but not until Thomas Tredwell rose on July 2 did a Bill of Rights get brought up. On July 7, John Lansing read the proposed Bill of Rights to the convention. Hamilton indicated in a letter to Madison that the Federalists were willing to make this concession in order to get the Constitution ratified, which is probably one of the reasons why the measure was successful.

In terms of the rights that were protected in the New York proposal, there was little difference between New York and Virginia. But there were some details in the language that were significant. The New York proposal stated, "That no person ought to be taken, imprisoned, or disseized of his freehold, or be exiled, or deprived of his privileges, franchises, life, liberty, or property, but by due process of law" (p. 912). By substituting "due process of law" for "law of the land," the New York document follows more accurately the language employed in Edward III's chapter 29 of the Magna Carta. The due process clause appeared for the first time in America in Massachusetts's Body of Liberties in 1641. But it was probably New York's proposal that led to the adoption of the language in the Fifth Amendment, which then led to the same language in the Fourteenth. Given the importance of the due process clause in the Supreme Court's protection of rights, the change of phrase was not trivial.

It is worth mentioning at least one other instance in which New York sought to protect property rights and to show that property, as in the other states, was considered both landed property and possessions:

That every freeman has a right to be secure from all unreasonable searches and seizures of his person, his papers, or his property; and therefore, that all warrants to search suspected places, or seize any freeman, his papers, or property, without information, upon oath or affirmation, of sufficient cause, are grievous and oppressive; and that all general warrants (or such in which the place or person suspected are not particularly designated) are dangerous, and ought not to be granted. (Schwartz 1971, p. 913)

Similar to the provisions found in the Virginia and national Bill of Rights, the delegates at the New York convention found it necessary to protect property, both landed and otherwise, from government infringement. In New York, and Virginia as well, the protection of property is aimed at thwarting government intervention, not invasion by private citizens, indicating that when it comes to rights, the government is considered a greater threat to one's rights. And this only stands to reason given that they just overthrew a government that did not respect their rights.

II. MADISON ON PROPERTY

Before one can accurately understand what the term *property* meant in the Bill of Rights, it is first necessary to understand what the term meant to the architect of the Bill of Rights. On a number of occasions, James Madison made his position on property known, without providing much detail. In a letter to Caleb Wallace, in 1785, Madison wrote, in reference to qualifications for elected officials, that "the rights of property which chiefly bears the burden of Government. . . ." (Madison 1999, p. 43). Madison's view on property and its relationship to government is uncomplicated; the chief duty of government is to protect property. The similarity to statements made by Locke are startling. Locke writes, "The great and chief end, therefore, of men's uniting into common-wealths and putting themselves under government, is the preservation of their property" (§124); which, when compared with Madison's comments in *Federalist* #10 and elsewhere, the similarity between the two becomes undeniable, which then reinforces just how influential Locke was on the founding generation as well as the primacy of property rights to our republican government.[5] But, it is still important to review why Madison makes the chief duty of government the preservation of property and the importance of property more generally. To answer these questions, it is first necessary to understand Madison's definition of property. Then, after defining property and the relationship between property and government, I will explore the proper balance between property and equality in Madison's thought. This section will provide the reader with a clear sense of what property is and why it is valuable, and to what extent it should be compromised in the pursuit of other values.

When read carefully, Madison indicates that the preservation to life, liberty, and property is the key to happiness and safety. "That government is instituted, and ought to be exercised for the benefit of the people; which consists in the enjoyment of life and liberty, with the right of acquiring and using property, and generally of pursuing and obtaining happiness and safety" (Schwartz 1971, p. 1026). Madison is saying that government is created for protection of those things that are naturally ours, and in protecting those things, we are aided in pursuing and obtaining happiness and safety. The point is obvious that a threat to one's life is a threat to his or her safety and happiness. A threat to one's liberty is a threat to the same, but primarily to happiness. Property is set off from liberty and life, but it is no less important to one's happiness and safety. And while his writings on property, to be discussed at length later, are helpful in interpreting this passage, just as instructive is a comment he made to Congress illustrating his general economic outlook:

> I own myself the friend to a very free system of commerce, and hold it as a truth, that commercial shackles are generally unjust, oppressive, and impolitic; it is also a truth, that if industry and labor are left to take their own course, they will generally be directed to those objects which are the most productive, and this in a more certain and direct manner than the wisdom of the most enlightened Legislature could point out. (Madison 1953, p. 269)

As property is the basis of a free economic order, and a free economic order is a desirable arrangement, then by extension, protecting private property is among the government's highest priorities. But because the government cannot, and should not, be relied upon, the people must retain this power. What follows is an analysis of Madison's specific remarks on property that support this conclusion.

II A. Definition of Property

Before any discussion moves too far along, the terms in the discussion must be clearly defined. For Madison, *property* has a dual meaning. Madison explicitly tells us how he defines property in an article published March 29, 1792, for the *National Gazette*. The first of his definitions is akin to Locke's, given at §32, and the second corresponds to what Locke asks us to infer:

> This term in its particular application means that dominion which one man claims and exercised over the external things of the world, in exclusion of every other individual. In its larger and juster meaning, it embraces every thing to which a man may attach a value and have a right; and which leaves every one else the like advantage. In the former sense, a man's land, or merchandize, or money is called his property. In the latter sense, a man has property in his opinions and the free communication of them. (Madison 1999, p. 515)

Madison is not far off from Locke in his conception of property. For Locke, each man possesses his labor, and whatever he mixes his labor with becomes his. For Madison, man has property in his material possessions and in himself. Madison does not speak of labor, but skips straight to property without explaining how one gains exclusivity over land or himself. In some sense, Locke's account is more detailed, but Madison's account explicitly includes those things that Locke only implies: "He has an equal property in the free use of his faculties and free choice of the objects on which to employ them. In a word, as a man is said to have a right to his property, he may be equally said to have a property in his rights" (Madison 1999, p. 515). Where Locke asks the reader to draw the conclusion that liberty and property are inseparably linked, which is why protection of property is the first object of government, Madison explicitly states that we have property in those rights that are inalienable. The government cannot take a citizen's right to free speech any more than it can take a citizen's land, simply because property is defined as something exclusive which one person, and only one person, can have dominion over.

Madison does not tell us how property comes to be; he only describes what it is and that it is of some value to the individual. For both Locke and Madison, property indicates exclusivity. My property is that which I have a right to for myself and can prevent others from having. While I cannot prevent others from having a free conscience, I can prevent them from having part of mine; just as I cannot take another person's land, they cannot take my land or my hog. Madison's definition of property includes a bundle of rights that are unalterable, inviolable, and exclusive to the individual. On this account, there is not much separation between Madison and Locke.

What is still unclear at this point is what type of property Madison had in mind when drafting what would become the Fifth Amendment. There are at least two possible ways of answering this question. First, it does not matter which property he was referring to, as material property flows from the free employment of one's faculties, which is also his property. Therefore, while Madison posits two definitions of property, it gives a false sense of duality. The two properties he refers to are, as Locke would have us conclude, inseparably linked. One cannot have security in his conscience without having security in his physical property. Positive laws ought to reflect natural law, which tells us that each individual has property in himself. Positive laws protecting physical property are only valid because they are derived from a natural law which says man has property in his own conscience, and his conscience—or faculties—is what leads to the physical property that is to be protected by positive law. Second, assuming a duality actually exists, Madison was referring to physical property in the Fifth Amendment, as the other type of property was the focus of the First Amendment. But even if one accepts that there are two separate definitions of property that are unrelated, it is still clear that Madison has an attachment to physical property that is undeniable. Furthermore, in his discussion of the value of physical property, he indicates that the relationship between the two types of property is one of interconnectedness rather than duality:

> If there be a government then which prides itself in maintaining the inviolability of property; which provides that none shall be taken directly even for public use without indemnification to the owner, and yet directly violates the property which individuals have in their opinions, their religion, their persons, and their faculties; nay more, which indirectly violates their property, in their actual possessions, in the labor that acquires their daily subsistence, and in the hallowed remnant of time which ought to relieve their fatigues and soothe their cares, the influence will have been anticipated, that such a government is not a pattern for the United States. (Madison 1999, p. 517)

Madison clearly thinks that a government that violates one property, while preserving another, is one that the United States should not become. The key to unlocking the connection between the two types of property lies in this passage when he suggests that the violation of an individual's opinion will indirectly violate his property in actual possession. The connection between the two types of property will be discussed throughout the remainder of this chapter; the aim here is to set the stage for that discussion by providing the two definitions of property Madison gives in order to shed light on what he meant by property in the Fifth Amendment. In any event, we will see a consistency between Madison, pre-Constitution America, and post-Constitution America in that the value of instrumental rights resides in their ability to protect property and that when considering property seizures, our modern government must overcome an enormous hurdle to justify its taking given the founding generation's attachment to property. The balance tips in the favor of property and is opposed to seizures—at least historically.

II B. Government and Property

"Government is instituted to protect property of every sort; as well as that which lies in the various rights of individuals, as that which the term particularly expresses" (Madison 1999, p. 515).[6] While how a government best protects property, and what constitutes a protection, are the central questions of this book, it is important to note that the protection of property is why government is instituted. This not only tells us that Madison considers property to be important, but that it is the reason government is instituted. Bad government is that government which exercises too much power over individual property, which then leads to insecurity and a loss of liberty (Madison 1999, p. 515).

But protecting property, though of paramount importance, is not an easy task, even in representative government. "The personal right to acquire property, which is a natural right, gives to property, when acquired, a right to protection, as a social right. The essence of Government is power; and power, lodged as it must be in human hands, will ever be liable to abuse" (Madison 1999, p. 825). Madison made this statement at the Virginia Constitutional Convention on December 2, 1829, which demonstrates his attachment to property rights even after the ratification of the Bill of Rights. This statement makes three interesting contributions. First, it moves the acquisition of property from a right protected by positive law to a natural law, which then places it alongside property of conscience in terms of priority. Second, it draws a link between property acquisition and safety as a social right, which demonstrates that, in properly constructed government, rights naturally possessed by the individual become rights granted to the entire society by positive law. Third, Madison admits that to protect these rights, the government must have power, for without power it has not authority. But, the power that is required to protect property is sufficient for destroying property; thus, the challenge becomes how to give a government enough energy to serve its purpose without overstepping its bounds. This is the topic visited by both Madison and Hamilton throughout the *Federalist Papers*.

Madison's *Federalist* #10 is well-known to almost everyone. His discussion of factions—and how their negative effects can be tempered without taking away liberty—is commonly discussed in introductory political science classes and in the scholarly literature. What garners less attention is the importance of property and its tie to liberty. Madison states, after listing the two methods for curing the mischiefs of faction, that there are two methods for removing the causes of faction: "The one by destroying the liberty which is essential to its existence; the other, by giving to every citizen the same opinions, the same passions, and the same interests" (#10: p. 43). Madison recommends neither of these: "It could never be more truly said that of the first remedy, that it is worse than the disease. Liberty is to faction, what air is to fire. . . . But it could not be a less folly to abolish liberty, which is essential to political life, because it nourishes faction, than it would be to wish the annihilation of air, which is essential to animal life because it imparts to fire its destructive agency" (#10: p. 43).

As for the second expedient, there is no doubt that it "is as impracticable, as the first would be unwise" (#10: p. 43). Man can never have the same interests; moreover, drawing on what was seen in his essay on property, it would be an invasion of man's liberty—equivalent to the first expedient of curing faction—because man's conscience is his property, and to force him to have the same opinion of everyone else would require an invasion of his property: "Conscience is the most sacred of all property; other property depending in part on positive law, the exercise of that, being a natural and unalienable right" (Madison 1999, p. 516). The second expedient is impractical, but to be successful it would require the government to employ the first expedient. Because man's opinions and passions will cloud his reason, thus making him biased in his own case, this gives rise to faction. To make man's opinions homogenous would be an unjust deprivation of property: "The diversity of faculties of men from which the rights of property originate, is not less an insuperable obstacle to an uniformity of interests. The protection of these faculties is the first object of government" (#10: p. 43).[7] This passage serves three purposes. First, it supports the argument that the two forms of property discussed by Madison in his "Property" essay only appear to be dual, and when considered carefully, the two forms of property are unified. The argument I made in the previous section was that physical property is derived from the property man has in his conscience, or mind. The statement from *Federalist* #10 supports that position. Second, it again restates the role of government. Whereas earlier it could have been said that preserving property is important, but it is not paramount. This statement clearly shows that a government that fails to provide protection of an individual's property has failed in its first duty as a government. Third, since the first object of government is the preservation of property, then it is rightly concluded that all other duties of government not connected to the preservation of property must be subservient to this first object. This has a direct bearing on cases of eminent domain. An individual's right to property trumps the government's ability to seize property. But because man's property is insecure without a government, property rights may be compromised if not doing so would lead to deterioration in the government's ability to protect property rights in the future. Madison has no doubt that giving everyone the same interests and the same opinion would serve the common good, but the common good is inferior to the preservation of "the diversity in the faculties of men from which the rights of property originate."

The third insight I draw is premised on the idea that government is better than no government except in the case where government makes property uncertain, thereby making no government and government indistinguishable. Madison demonstrates this point in his critique of democracies. Democracies offer no cure for factions because a common passion may overtake the whole and threaten the common good. If the common good is threatened, presumably private rights will be as well. "Hence it is, that such democracies have ever been spectacles of turbulence and contention; have ever been found incompatible with personal security, or the rights of property; and have in general been as short in their lives, as they have been violent in their deaths" (#10: p. 46). Not only do governments that fail to provide the first object of government fail in general, but they do so violently. Also, as discussed at the beginning of this subsection, personal security—not just personal liberty—is tied to personal property rights. Safety and liberty are linked in that safety without liberty is worthless, and liberty without safety cannot exist. Therefore, property, while an exhibition of liberty, is also a protector of liberty, which is why personal security is used synonymously with rights of property.

II C. Property and Equality

Locke and Madison recognize that when private property is protected, inequality will result. Different people have different ambitions and capabilities—what Madison refers to in #10 as a "diversity of faculties"—which will result in different levels of property accumulation. For Madison, this is problematic because it causes a rise in factions. Madison is not alone in his concern about economic disparity. But Madison does recognize that to enforce equality of property ownership would be to infringe on property rights. As already discussed, Madison recognizes that to deprive men of their property is to rob them of their liberty, and to make men equal in terms of property would require the government to strip them of those things that government was originally formed to protect. The tension that exists between property and the common good in contemporary discussions did not exist at the time of the founding, as it was recognized by that generation that the common good is dependent upon the protection of private property. This point, in addition to what has already been said, finds support in Madison's discussion of property and equality.

In some instances, Madison is ambiguous in his promotion of property over equality. Because he recognizes the damage factions can do, and he recognizes that factions arise from disproportionate levels of property ownership, which is the result of men being unequal in their faculties, Madison does recognize the need for government to promote some level of equality among its citizens. In a *National Gazette* article titled "Parties," published January 23, 1792, Madison writes, "By the silent operation of laws, which, without violating the rights of property, reduce extreme wealth towards a state of mediocrity, and raise extreme indigence towards a state of comfort" (Madison 1999, p. 504). This might have the reader suppose that equality is an object of government that warrants some amount of property right infringement. At some point, it could be concluded that even Madison recognized that the public good requires the refusal of property acquisition and accumulation to some, despite what he has consistently said to the contrary. However, this would be a false conclusion. If we assume that Madison held similar views to others in the state ratification conventions who argued for an amendment protecting property rights, then, as has been shown, the preservation of the public good is second to the protection of private property. This assumption is justified when one reads carefully what

Madison wrote in 1792 as he recommends the promotion of equality with respect to property rights. Even though inequality is damaging to the political order, violating rights of property would be worse. The ambiguity that seems to exist in Madison's essay on parties never appears in any of his others writings, which means we may safely conclude that when equality and property come into conflict, the government must decide in favor of property.

In his "Property" essay, published only a few months after his "Parties" essay, Madison writes, "Government is instituted to protect property of every sort. . . . This being the end of government, that alone is a *just* government, which *impartially* secures to every man, whatever is his *own*" (Madison 1999, p. 515; italics Madison's). When it comes to the protection of property rights, the government cannot favor one faction over another, nor is it recommended—or even conceivable—that there be an ideological divide among those in government over the importance of property. There has been no evidence to suggest that there were dissenters on the issue of private property protection. While two of the proposed amendments were not ratified, indicating there was some dissension on some issues, property had unanimous support. This is indicated not only by Madison's full-throated support, but in the House and Senate debates in which no dissenting view was expressed over the eminent domain provision recommended by Madison.

In the "Property" essay, Madison argues, "That is not a just government, nor is property secure under it, where the property which a man has in his person of safety and personal liberty, is violated by arbitrary seizures of one class of citizens for the service of the rest" (Madison 1999, p. 516). I do not want to paint too sympathetic a picture of Madison and suggest he is making an argument against slavery; rather he is merely restating a point Locke had already made (§§11–13). It can be read that Madison is suggesting that where property is not secure, nothing is secure. This is true, but oversimplified in the fact that the separation between property, safety, and liberty is truly nonexistent. Property—whether conscience or landed—is the realization of liberty. To have property, and thus liberty, one must also have safety. But one cannot be safe without liberty, thus making property vital for safety as well, because it is the ability to realize one's liberty that places the ultimate check on government. Thus, there is a unity of rights.

Madison reiterates this point in the next paragraph of his essay when he writes:

> That is not a government, nor is property secure under it, where the arbitrary restrictions, exemptions, and monopolies deny to part of its citizens that free use of their faculties, and free choice of their occupations, which not only constitute their property in the general sense of the word; but are the means of acquiring property strictly so called. (Madison 1999, p. 516)

There is no ambiguity in this statement. Moreover, the relationship between the two definitions of property, liberty, and safety is clearly stated.

Madison has clearly indicated his attachment to property and the reasons for it. To deprive one of property is to deprive one of liberty and safety, the preservation of which is the sole purpose of government; thus, a government that infringes on one's property, infringes on one's liberty and safety, thus rendering it not a government. But that does not resolve the problem of deciding to what degree equality ought to be sacrificed for property or how property provides for the public good to a greater degree than equality.

> From the protection of different and unequal faculties of acquiring property, the possession of different degrees and kinds of property immediately results: And from the influence of these on the sentiments and views of the respective proprietors, ensues a division of the society into different interests and parties. . . . But the most common and durable source of factions has been the various and unequal distribution of property. Those who hold, and those who are without property, have ever formed distinct interests in society. Those who are creditors, and those who are debtors, fall under like discrimination. A landed interest, a manufacturing interest, a mercantile interest, a monied interest, with many lesser interests, grow up of necessity in civilized nations, and divide them into different classes, actuated by different sentiments and views. The regulation of these various and interfering interests forms the principal task of modern legislation, and involves the spirit of party and faction in the necessary and ordinary operations of government. (#10: p. 43, 44)

Madison clearly understands that property ownership leads to one of the most persistent problems in governance. But as he stated earlier in the essay, you cannot get rid of property or the source of the inequality of property without first destroying liberty, which he readily admits is a solution worse than the problem. Moreover, eliminating factions is impossible, even if we were willing to sacrifice liberty and safety, because "The latent causes of faction are thus sown in the nature of man. . . ." (#10: p. 43). So not only is eliminating faction undesirable, it is impossible, which means the solution lies in controlling factions and not eliminating them (#10: p. 45). Implicit in his solution is the recognition that property is more valuable than equality, for if it were not, there would be no problem extinguishing the source of faction.

Not only is Madison unwilling to sacrifice liberty for equality, but that sacrifice would not result in the reduction of factions. In his critique of democracies, Madison writes, "Theoretic politicians, who have patronized this species of government, have erroneously supposed, that, by reducing mankind to a perfect equality in their political rights, they would, at the same time, be perfectly equalized and assimilated in their possessions, their opinions, and their passions" (#10: p. 46). Thinking that the pursuit of equality holds the key to solving the ills of government is, in Madison's words, erroneous. This is why he argues for a republic and not a democracy. The public good is not preserved or achieved by the promotion of equality, rather it is only through the promotion of property—which entails a promotion of safety and liberty. The promotion of equality at the expense of property calls for a restriction of liberty and is therefore a threat to safety. But more than erroneous, the restriction on property rights is wicked, "a rage for paper money, for an abolition of debts, for an equal division of property, or for any other improper or wicked project, will be less apt to pervade the whole body of the union. . . ." (#10: p. 48). Therefore, liberty—and by extension property—ought not to be sacrificed for equality, because the public good is achieved not through equality but through liberty and safety. The promotion of equality at the expense of property threatens the public good.

For Madison, and for others, there is no tradeoff between property, liberty, and safety as they are interdependent. Sacrificing one would be sacrificing the others. This has been seen in Madison's comments, as well as those politicians in the founding era that treated instrumental and intrinsic rights along the same dimension. The phenomenon of splitting economic rights from other rights came after the founding generation passed. The politicization of these rights, by placing one set of rights with one political party and the other set with the other, represents a profound misunderstanding of these rights and a break with the founding, thereby increasing the risk of losing these rights.

> If the United States mean to obtain or deserve the full praise due to wise and just governments, they will equally respect rights of property, and the property in rights: they will rival the government that most sacredly guards the former; and by repelling its example in violating the latter, will make themselves a pattern to that and all other governments. (Madison 1999, p. 517)

III. LEGISLATIVE HISTORY AND RATIFICATION BY THE STATES

As discussed earlier, one of the original concerns of the Anti-Federalists and the state ratifying conventions was the lack of a Bill of Rights in the new Constitution. On June 8, 1789, in the House of Representatives, James Madison, Congressman from Virginia, introduced amendments to the Constitution designed to protect the rights of citizens. After going through the committee process, on October 2, 1789, the amendments were submitted to the states for approval. This move was designed to put at ease the concerns of the two states—North Carolina and Rhode Island—who had yet to ratify the Constitution and to appease those states—Massachusetts, South Carolina, New Hampshire, Virginia, and New York—who submitted their own amendments at the time of ratification. While the process was one of compromise forced by committee work, the final product still embodied most of Madison's original proposal.

Coming from one of the most contentious states, and having played a vital role in gaining the ratification of Virginia as a delegate and New York as one-third of Publius, Madison was well positioned to have success in proposing amendments. Not only did he have the backing of one of the strongest states in the Union, but he was also—prior to ratification—a Federalist pushing an Anti-Federalist proposal. When Madison spoke on the floor of the House on June 8, 1789, he presented amendments to the Constitution that were to be added to the body of the document, not a Bill of Rights, as we now know it. The amendments he proposed reflected the recommendations of the five states that made recommendations and the recommendations of the two remaining holdouts. Madison was not entirely successful as only ten of the original twelve amendments were ratified by the states initially. The first proposed amendment focused on the ratio between citizens and representatives was not ratified as part of the Bill of Rights, and the second proposed amendment which dealt with congressional compensation was not ratified until 1992 as the 27th Amendment.

Originally, the amendment that we now recognize as the Fifth, Madison recommended be included in Article 1, Section 9, between clauses 3 and 4. Madison proposed the following:

> No person shall be subject, except in cases of impeachment, to more than one punishment or one trial for the same offence; nor shall be compelled to be a witness against himself; nor be deprived of life, liberty, or property, without due process of law; nor be obliged to relinquish his property, where it may be necessary for public use, without a just compensation. (Schwartz 1971, p. 1027)

Accompanying these provisions were others that would be found throughout the Bill of Rights.

On July 28, 1789, amendments were reported to the House Select Committee. The revised version included only a minor revision of Madison's proposal. Where Madison wrote, "nor be obliged to relinquish his property, where it may be necessary for public use, without a just compensation," the new version read, "nor shall private property be taken for public use without just compensation" (Levy 1999, p. 285). In both versions, the only means by which private property could be taken was through the due process of law, in which the person would have been accused of a crime or, in the case of public use, for which the property holder would receive just compensation.

After coming back from the Select Committee, the House passed an identical version of the Select Committee version on August 24, 1789. The provision on private property was in the Eighth Amendment, but due to the first two amendments not being ratified and the Third and Fourth eventually being collapsed into one amendment, the Eight Amendment, as passed by the House, is today's Fifth, relatively unchanged. Once passed through the House, the Senate passed its own set of amendments on September 9, 1789. In the Senate's version, the House's Fourth and Third were collapsed into one amendment and more stipulations were placed upon rights to jury trials and grand jury indictments, but the language dealing with property remained unchanged.

The conference that met on September 25, after the amendments passed through both houses, approved of the changes made by the Senate and sent to the states twelve amendments to be ratified, with the amendment containing the property provisions in the seventh position.

Once the amendments were sent to the states, ratification was rapid. In Massachusetts, the House and Senate journals report that the amendments were received on January 28, and approved—with the exception of the first and second—on February 2nd (Schwartz 1971, p. 1177). In New York, it took from October 29 to January 26 to approve the amendments. The increased time resulted from having the amendments sent around to various towns for consideration prior to legislative action. There was little doubt that once powers such as Virginia, New York, and Pennsylvania ratified the new documents, the rest of the states would follow. There is clear evidence to suggest that both politicians and citizens were aware of what was going on in the other states as newspaper accounts of the status of the amendments in other states were common. Only six states—Maryland, North Carolina, Rhode Island, South Carolina, Vermont, and Virginia—ratified all of the amendments which meant only the last ten were passed.

On March 1, 1792, Thomas Jefferson—then Secretary of State under George Washington—wrote a letter to the President officially announcing the ratification of the amendments:

Sir,
I have the honor to send you herein enclosed, two copies duly authenticated, of and Act concerning certain fisheries of the United States, and for the regulation and government of fishermen employed therein; also of an Act to establish the post office and post roads within the United States; also the ratifications by three-fourths of the Legislatures of the Several States, of certain articles in addition and amendment of the Constitution of the United States, proposed by Congress to the said Legislatures, and of being with sentiments of the most perfect respect, your Excellency's &.

Th. Jefferson

Modern readers surely find Jefferson's letter humorous in its ability to remain reserved and to understate such a profound event. The announcement did not even warrant a letter of its own. He either did not see the historical significance or assumed that Washington was already aware of the occurrence and was simply reporting the events as part of his duty. In either case, what occurred in the first Congress and in the states would forever shape American politics, whether Jefferson recognized it at the time or not.

SUMMARY

The ratification of the Bill of Rights led similar language to be adopted in the state constitutions of Pennsylvania in 1790, South Carolina in 1790, Kentucky in 1792, Tennessee in 1796, Mississippi in 1817, Illinois in 1818, and Ohio in 1802. While the genesis of property rights in America is found in English common law and John Locke as transmitted through state declarations, after the ratification of the national Bill of Rights, the message was sent to the states by the federal government that these rights are fundamental.

In summarizing Madison's role in developing a national understanding of property rights, James Ely writes:

> In addition, Madison addressed the question of taking private property for public use. Stressing "the inviolability of property," he noted that property could not be "directly" taken without just compensation. Madison further declared that a government "which indirectly violates their property, in actual possessions . . . is not a pattern for the United States." Because the value of property can be diminished by governmental action short of actual seizure, Madison's reference to indirect infringement indicates a generous understanding of the takings clause to encompass more than just the physical taking of property. (Ely 1998, p. 56)

If we base what we know on speeches, other historical evidence, and philosophical justifications, it seems reasonable to conclude that the attachment to property by the founding generation was great, and therefore, deprivation of property could only be done in the most extreme circumstances given the inherent risk and deleterious effect it would have on the preservation of their liberty. Extrapolating from that, the benefit of confiscating property must be demonstrably greater than not, and the public use must be real and direct. Therefore, property can only be seized when the survival of the government depends upon it.

This chapter has reinforced the position that the founding generation considered rights unified and did not consider rights along ideological dimensions. This unity is clearly embodied in the Fifth Amendment as seen through its historical origins and literary construction.

NOTES

1. Amar argues that Madison tried to sneak property protection into the Bill of Rights by placing it in the middle of the Fifth Amendment. The most obvious objection to this point goes unaddressed by Amar. Due to its simplicity, it does not need to be discussed at much length here either. First, not all of the Amendments proposed by Madison were ratified. Second, the structure of Madison's proposal was dramatically altered in its final version. If Madison's plan was to sneak something through, it obviously would have been a bad plan given that each state, the Congress as a whole, and various committees in the Congress had a say in its final construction. Do we really think that Madison thought he could get this through so many checkpoints without anyone noticing? While these observations go far in rebuffing Amar, they do not make a substantive contribution to the debate over the value of property rights, their relation to the other provisions in the Fifth Amendment, or Madison's position on property. This chapter, and book, is dedicated to advancing all three of those points. This chapter will demonstrate (1) there was a dual meaning to property, which makes it entirely appropriate to include property in the Fifth Amendment, and (2) as was shown in an earlier chapter, the value of procedural due process rights is founded in their ability to protect life, liberty, and property.

2. Oddly, Madison had earlier opposed a Bill of Rights. But, this does not mean his thought on the matter should be discounted. His earlier opposition does not mean he was insincere in formulating the Bill of Rights. Moreover, Madison is not the only important founder when it comes to understanding property rights. But given that he was the chief architect of the Bill of Rights and played the most influential role in ushering them through Congress, his thought on the matter deserves an extended treatment and attention.

3. All page numbers that accompany state documents refer to Schwartz 1971, Volume 2.

4. Federalists included Alexander Hamilton, John Jay, and Robert Livingston. The Anti-Federalists had George Clinton, John Lansing, and Melancton Smith.

5. In addition to chapter 2 of this book, one should also recall Locke's §3, "Political power, then, I take to be a right to make laws with penalties of death, and consequently all less penalties, for the regulating and preserving of property, and of employing the force of the community, in the execution of such laws, and in the defence of the common-wealth from foreign injury; and all this only for the public good."

6. Remember Locke who writes, "The great and chief end, therefore, of men uniting into common-wealths, and putting themselves under government, is the preservation of property" (§124).

7. As I have demonstrated, there are numerous places in which Madison states the end of government is the preservation of property even though property is the source of faction. But to push the point further, in a letter to Jefferson, Madison writes, "A distinction of property results from that very protection which a free Government gives to unequal faculties of acquiring it" (24 October 1787, *Founder's Constitution*, Vol. 1, chapter 17, Document 22).

Chapter 5

Examining the Decisions

The 2004–2005 Supreme Court term saw three property rights cases decided, *Lingle v. Chevron*,[1] *San Remo Hotel v. City and County of San Francisco*,[2] and *Kelo v. City of New London*.[3] *San Remo* considered whether claims against regulatory takings could be taken to federal court; in *Lingle*, the Court considered when a taking affects a Fifth Amendment taking; and in *Kelo*, the Court gave authority to state and local governments to use the power of eminent domain to transfer property from one private property owner to another. Each of these cases illustrates the Court's trend of loosening the protections afforded to property owners. Both *San Remo* and *Lingle* deal with important issues, but *Kelo* represents the most profound statement of the Court's position on property rights, and thus will receive more attention than the others in this chapter. These decisions did not set new precedents in property rights jurisprudence; instead, they follow a recent trend in the Court's curtailment of property rights. As James Ely writes, "the Court followed its recent trend of curtailing ownership rights in the face of economic regulations and governmental acquisition by eminent domain . . . property rights . . . are ending . . . with a whimper, not a bang" (Ely 2005a, p. 39; footnote omitted).

Sympathizers of the Court's position on property rights have characterized—correctly at times—critics of the Court as going overboard (Burke 2006, p. 704). Cass Sunstein writes that those efforts to retrench the preservation of property rights in the Constitution have done so to the detriment of a correct reading of the Constitution as they try "to reinvigorate the Constitution's Takings Clause to insulate property rights from democratic control" (Sunstein 2005, p. 10). What Sunstein's criticism misses is that property rights enhance democracy by promoting economic and political

87

stability. Moreover, the Constitution was designed as an instrument of checks and balances, not democratic control. Burke criticizes those who want to replace the presumption of constitutionality with the presumption of liberty (Burke 2006, p. 704). Both she and her targets—if she has properly characterized them—are misguided on this matter. There is no distinction between the Constitution and liberty, especially after the Bill of Rights was added. The Constitution, in the Preamble, sets up a number of important goals for itself, but based upon the discussion that took place in the previous chapters, all of those goals are linked, if not reliant upon, the "blessings of liberty." Burke's misreading is a common reading among scholars. This misreading of our constitutional heritage has caused a sharp divide among scholars. Burke and others characterize those who favor property rights as wanting to return to the *Lochner*-era, and those who are the targets of this criticism see the competing position as a threat to constitutionally protected rights. What was a relevant academic debate has turned into ideological banter because both sides see rights as political matters that fall on different sides of an ideological divide. The debate has stalled. Once the origin of the Fifth Amendment is correctly understood—as attempted in chapter 4— both sides will see that property rights are intimately related with other rights, and the protection of—or destruction of—property rights will have the same impact on the other rights, and even if not immediate, the effects will be felt across the board. Building on the previous chapters, I will develop in this chapter a critique of the *Kelo* decision that will bridge the ideological gap. I have no doubt that I will abandon the extremes on both sides, but I have confidence that the sensible members of each camp will come to appreciate the value of all rights and see *Kelo* as a threat to more than property.

The right of a sovereign to exercise eminent domain precedes the United States and the colonies. While chapter 1 showed how eminent domain evolved in English common law, the concept of compensating property owners for a government taking extends as far back as the Roman Empire (Kotlyarevskaya 2006, p. 199). When government seizes property, it must be done according to the due process of law, public use, public good, and the owner must be justly compensated. Only *San Remo* will be considered explicitly under the due process prong, but each of the three cases could be seen as a violation of due process if public use and public good are not present. I will consider whether the public use and public good requirements were met in the *Kelo* decision, and I will critique the decision on incorporation grounds in that the decision did not properly incorporate the Fifth Amendment. "Because the Fifth Amendment applies to all states through the Fourteenth Amendment 'there is a possibility of a federal question in every taking by eminent domain under state authority, even if all requirements of the constitution of the state are held to have been complied with'" (Kotlyarevskaya 2006, p. 199; footnote omitted). It is not that the Court did not consider the Fifth Amendment applicable to the states, but the Court did not apply it to the states; it decided to let the states decide for themselves whether they would uphold the Court's reading of the Fifth Amendment. And while I do not want to see the Court's reading enforced upon the states, this is yet one other avenue by which one can demonstrate the faulty logic of the Court and its failure to appreciate our constitutional heritage:

I. *LINGLE V. CHEVRON*

While *Kelo* gets most of the attention from the media, politicians, and citizens, Martha Burke argues that, "The Supreme Court also decided another land use case that term, *Lingle v. Chevron*, which went a long way in clarifying the Court's takings jurisprudence under the Fifth Amendment. Arguably *Lingle* is a much more important case jurisprudentially than *Kelo*. . . ." (Burke 2006, p. 665).

There are approximately three hundred different service stations in Hawaii, about half of which are leased from oil companies by independent lessee-dealers. Chevron sells most of its product in Hawaii through independent lessee-dealers in which Chevron buys the land from a third party, builds a service station, and then leases the service station to another party. Chevron requires the lessee to buy and sell its product and charges the lessee rent. In June 1997, the Hawaii Legislature passed Act 257, which restricted, among other things, the amount of rent Chevron could charge its lessees. Chevron sued Hawaii, claiming that the rent cap affected a taking of Chevron's property and thus violated the Fifth and Fourteenth Amendments. Chevron sought summary judgment and an injunction against the application of the rent cap. Each side agreed that the Act reduced the amount of aggregate rent due to Chevron by $207,000 per year. The district court granted summary judgment to Chevron, holding that Act 257 failed to advance a legitimate state interest, thus it is an unconstitutional taking. The Ninth Circuit Court of Appeals vacated the grant of summary judgment on the ground that a genuine issue of material fact still remained as to whether the Act would benefit consumers, thus advancing a legitimate state interest. On remand, the district court held again for Chevron, and this time the Ninth Circuit affirmed.

In its decision, written by Sandra Day O'Connor, the Supreme Court decided that an inquiry into whether a state action substantially advances a state interest, as established in *Agins v. Tiburon*,[4] is not a valid takings test, thus overturning the lower court's opinion:

> Twenty-five years ago, the Court posited that a regulation of private property "affects a taking if it does not substantially advance a legitimate state interest." The lower courts in this case took that statement to its logical conclusion, and in so doing, revealed its imprecision. Today we correct course. We hold that the "substantially advances" formula is not a valid takings test, and indeed conclude that it has no proper place in our takings jurisprudence. In so doing, we reaffirm that a plaintiff seeking to challenge a government regulation as an uncompensated taking of private property may proceed under one of the other theories discussed above—by alleging a "physical" taking, a *Lucas*-type "total regulatory taking," a *Penn Central* taking, or a land-use exaction violating the standards set forth in *Nollan* and *Dolan*. Because Chevron argued only a "substantially advances" theory in support of its takings claim, it was not entitled to summary judgment on that claim. Accordingly, we reverse the judgment of the Ninth Circuit and remand the case for further proceedings consistent with this opinion. (*Lingle v. Chevron*, 2005, 125 U.S. at 2087)

While the Court did allow Chevron to raise its claim again on constitutionally justifiable grounds, it seems that *Lingle* is still a setback.[5]

Quite simply, in *Lingle*, the Court seemed confused. In *Penn Central, Lucas, Nollan*, and *Dolan*, the Court dealt with a variety of takings issues, therefore invoking all of them for the same purpose is a bit of a reach. *Penn Central* was the precedent the Court primarily relied on for its reasoning in *Lingle* (Burke 2006; Ely 2005a). But the question raised in *Penn Central* was substantially different from the one raised in *Lingle*. In *Lingle*, the Court effectively addressed a different question than the one raised at the lower court level. *Penn Central* raised the question of what constituted a taking, not whether a taking was legitimate. In *Lingle*, neither side was disputing that there was a taking, nor was Chevron seeking compensation. At the district court level, both sides agreed that there was a taking and that Chevron would be negatively affected. Thus, whether it was a taking that was not in dispute, the Supreme Court decided the case as though this was in dispute. It seems the Court decided to reinterpret the facts of the case on appeal, or at least change the question it was being asked to consider. Moreover, in *Penn Central*, the plaintiff was seeking compensation under the Fifth Amendment. In a number of instances in *Lingle*, O'Connor raised the issue of just compensation, thus it appears that question colored her judgment in the case. This is only problematic because Chevron was not asking for compensation, only an injunction. Despite her otherwise conflicting statements, O'Connor did admit that Chevron did not seek compensation, but only an injunction, thereby requiring the Court to review a wide array of state and federal statutes, thus violating the deferential treatment generally given to economic legislation (*Lingle v. Chevron*, 2005, 125 U.S. at 2085; see also Ely 2005a, p. 51). It is not clearly stated by the majority why they felt the need to defer to the legislature in this instance, as the questions of public good and public use that usually call for such deference were not the primary questions in the case. It seems the Court failed to fulfill its constitutional responsibility of checking the legislative branch. Certainly the legislative branch should be granted latitude to enact legislation within its expertise and germane to its constitutionally prescribed role, but that does not mean the Court should not hold the legislative branch accountable for unconstitutional actions.

The objections I have raised to the decision have not been raised previously, but there have been equally valid criticisms of the Court's decision developed elsewhere that do not conflict with mine. Ely makes the argument that the Court's recommendation that the issue be raised again by Chevron on due process grounds is "fanciful" because there is no reason to think that the Court would grant a property rights review under due process given O'Connor's claim that the Court ought to defer to the legislature on questions of economic regulation (Ely 2005a, p. 52). O'Connor writes, "Reading it to demand heightened means ends review of virtually all regulation of private property would require courts to scrutinize the efficacy of a vast array of state and federal regulations—a task for which they are not well-suited" (*Lingle v. Chevron*, 2005, 125 U.S. at 2085). Ely's concern is valid; if the Court has concluded that it is not well-suited to scrutinize regulations in one instance, then certainly it would conclude the same in another. Ely's central concern regarding this facet of the decision is reflected in a similar concern that runs throughout this book. Except for property rights, the Court has decided that it should extend its ability to protect all rights. The Court sees property rights as distinct from other rights and has left property rights to the legislature, while shuddering at the thought of leaving questions of abortion, school prayer, or free speech in the hands of legislators. My concern parallels Ely's, but I do not seek to lay the blame at the feet of the New Deal Court for this departure. While I admit that the New Deal exemplifies a change in our constitutional history, I simply do not think that it is the beginning of the change (Scott 2008, chapter 6; see also Carrese 2003). Moreover, I think there is more at stake than Ely realizes. Ely has rightly concerned himself with the loss of property rights for their own sake. While I suggest that a loss of property rights is inherently bad, what the loss means for all rights makes the trend all the worse.

Ely recognizes a silver lining in the *Lingle* decision in that it helps clarify what constitutes a taking. But the problem is that the Court still places its definition of a taking on other opinions which themselves rest on shaky ground. The only remedy seems to be for the Court to revisit the Constitution on its own merits.

II. *SAN REMO HOTEL V. CITY AND COUNTY OF SAN FRANCISCO*

Hoteliers in San Francisco sought to convert residential rooms into tourist rooms. For the conversion to be allowed, the owners of the San Remo Hotel would have to pay a fee of $567,000 to San Francisco. Unsurprisingly, the hotel owners challenged this law as a regulatory taking. The petitioners initially filed for mandamus in California state court, but the action was stayed when the petitioners filed suit in federal district court challenging the statute's constitutionality under the Fifth Amendment's Takings Clause. The district court granted summary judgment to the city on the grounds that the case was not ripe, and the Ninth Circuit Court affirmed the district court's ruling on the issue of ripeness even though it abstained from ruling because of the pending state mandamus. Forced to return to the state court, the petitioners' claims were rejected, forcing them to return to district court now that they had satisfied what they thought were the requirements for ripeness after having exhausted the state's available remedies. But because the federal district court was asked to hear the identical claims raised at the state level, the district court decided that the case was barred by rule of issue preclusion. The petitioner's request to exempt federal takings from the reach of the full faith and credit statute was denied. Both the Ninth Circuit Court and the Supreme Court agreed with the district court's ruling. The litigation of this case created a scenario one would have thought was right out of the mind of Joseph Heller.[6] In the simplest terms possible: the Court decided that in order for a takings case to be ripe it must first be heard at the state level, but if the same claims are made at the federal level as were made at the state level, the case cannot be heard at the federal level because of the full faith and credit statute.

The Court relied on *Williamson County Regional Planning Commission v. Hamilton Bank of Johnston City*[7] to make its decision. The two-pronged test developed in *Williamson County,* which requires that a claimant must obtain a final decision on his or her land use application at the state level and for the claimant to have sought and been denied compensation at the state level, was applied in *San Remo.* While Rehnquist decided in the majority, in his concurring opinion, he did question the validity of the second prong of the *Williamson County* test:

It is not clear to me that *Williamson County* was correct in demanding that, once a government entity has reached a final decision with respect to a claimant's property, the claimant must seek compensation in state court before bringing a federal takings claim in federal court. The Court in *Williamson County* purported to interpret the Fifth Amendment in divining this state-litigation requirement. . . . It is not obvious that either constitutional or prudential principles require claimants to utilize all state compensation procedures before they can bring a federal takings claim. . . . Finally, *Williamson County's* state-litigation rule has created some real anomalies, justifying our revisiting the issue. For example, our holding today ensures that litigants who go to state court to seek compensation will likely be unable later to assert their federal takings claims in federal court. . . . And, even if preclusion law would not block a litigant's claim, the *Rooker-Feldman* doctrine might, insofar as *Williamson County* can be read to characterize the state courts' denial of compensation as a required element of the Fifth Amendment takings claim. . . . As the Court recognizes, *Williamson County* all but guarantees that claimants will be unable to utilize the federal courts to enforce the Fifth Amendment's just compensation guarantee. (*San Remo v. City and County of San Francisco,* 2005, 125 S. Ct. at 2508–2510)

Unfortunately, Rehnquist's concern did not matter in this particular case, given the narrow grant of *certiorari* in *San Remo.*

The *Rooker-Feldman* doctrine Rehnquist refers to states that only the Supreme Court could entertain a proceeding to reverse or modify a state court judgment. This doctrine was expanded during the civil rights era by federal courts seeking to dismiss hundreds of civil rights cases coming from the state level (Lewis and Norman 2004, p. 429). Thus, the threat to rights posed by *San Remo* is hardly alarmist.

Because federal courts lack the expertise of state courts when it comes to takings claims, and there is scant precedent for takings claims in federal district court, Justice Stevens, writing for the majority, decided to reject the petitioners' claim to grant an exception to the full faith and credit statute for takings claims. But, Stevens and the majority do not consider the problem raised by Rehnquist, and the effect is that state claimants now lack a federal outlet for their takings claims. It appears that the Court manufactured ripeness test supersedes constitutional considerations raised under the Fourteenth Amendment and the Bill of Rights.

Justice Stevens's claim that the Court cannot overrule a federal statute that stands in the way of guaranteeing due process to takings plaintiffs is unfounded (*San Remo v. City and County of San Francisco,* 2005, 125 S. Ct. at 2504). Since *Marbury v. Madison, Martin v. Hunter's Lessee,* and the Judiciary Act of 1789, the Court and Congress have recognized Stevens's claim as false. Moreover, Article VI, Clause 2 of the Constitution reads,

"This Constitution, and the Laws of the United States which shall be made in Pursuance thereof . . . shall be the supreme Law of the land . . ." Laws must be made pursuant of the Constitution, the Constitution should not be subjected to a legislative determination of the public good. The Judiciary Act of 1789 and *Martin v. Hunter's Lessee* both establish a legal hierarchy in which the U.S. Constitution is above federal statute, and *Marbury v. Madison* is the most famous judicial manifestation of this hierarchy by establishing judicial authority to overturn a federal statute on constitutional grounds. Stevens seems to be grasping at straws, though it is unclear why there were no dissenters on the Court unless we say that the judges felt so constrained by federal statute, precedent, and the narrow grant of *certiorari* that they could not have decided otherwise. That is, the Court is not activist at all. But, what the Court was being asked to do was protect property rights in a manner consistent with how it has chosen to protect other rights. To this end, the petitioners in *San Remo* were denied the protection of their rights because they were asking for the protection of property and not speech, religion, or some other right the Court has decided is worth protecting.

The reach of this case goes beyond the parties in *San Remo*. The Court has effectively rendered takings cases a state matter, which is consistent with the *Kelo* decision, but inconsistent with the incorporation cases that have sought to extend the Bill of Rights to the states. The Court has effectively limited protections to property owners under the Fifth Amendment to cases in which the federal government is a party.

III. *KELO V. CITY OF NEW LONDON*

This section will begin with a description of the case and provide a brief analysis of the majority opinion. Then, the section will provide a more detailed critique of the Court's definition of public use, public good, and its failure to extend Fifth Amendment protections to the states.

III A. The Case and Brief Analysis

In 2000, the city of New London, Connecticut, sought to increase jobs and revitalize its waterfront and downtown areas by adopting a development plan that required the city to seize private property. The city's proposal included building hotels, restaurants, movie theaters, a river walk, new residences, retail and office space, and other office and research facilities. The Fort Trumbull area, which was about ninety acres, was targeted by the city for this redevelopment. Rather than the city developing and carrying out the plan, the New London Development Corporation (NLDC) was established. The NLDC was a private, nonprofit entity that took the helm of the development efforts. After the plan had been approved by numerous state and local agencies, the city granted the NLDC the right to seize private property via eminent domain.[8] Susette Kelo, who had lived in Fort Trumbull since 1997, was unwilling to sell her home, and the NLDC used eminent domain to seize it.[9] After winning a seven-day trial in the city of New London Superior Court, and losing in the Supreme Court of Connecticut, Susette Kelo appealed to the U.S. Supreme Court which then upheld the decision of the Supreme Court of Connecticut in a 5–4 ruling.

The Fifth Amendment stipulates that eminent domain requires the state to provide just compensation for seized property and that it is done for the public use. Kelo did not dispute the seizure on grounds of just compensation, but insisted that the land was not being taken for public use because the property was being developed and seized by a private developer, and some of the land would not be made accessible to the general public; and she contested whether a predicted benefit that was purely economic—meaning an increased tax base—could be considered a public good. The Court had to decide on each of these matters and dispense with them dutifully in order to allow Kelo's home to be seized by NLDC.

Writing for the majority, Justice Stevens wrote:

> Given the comprehensive character of the plan, the thorough deliberation that preceded its adoption, and the limited scope of our review, it is appropriate for us, as it was in *Berman,* to resolve the challenges of the individual owners, not on a piecemeal basis, but rather in light of the entire plan. Because that plan unquestionably serves a public purpose, the takings challenged here satisfy the public use requirement of the Fifth Amendment. (*Kelo v. City of New London,* 2005, 125 S. Ct. at 2655)

It seems Fort Trumbull being a blighted area played into the Court's decision to side with the NLDC (*Kelo v. City of New London,* 2005, 125 S. Ct. at 2665, 2666, 2669), which makes their renovation plan appropriate, even though the Court admits that

> There is no allegation that any of these properties is blighted or otherwise in poor condition; rather, they were condemned only because they happen to be located in the development area. . . . Those who govern the City were not confronted with the need to remove blight in the Fort Trumbull area, but their determination that the area was sufficiently distressed to justify a program of economic rejuvenation is entitled to our deference. (*Kelo v. City of New London,* 2005, 125 S. at Ct. 2661)

Therefore, there was no evidence offered by the respondent that the areas were blighted or in need of renovation, only that there was a plan proposed that would be more economically beneficial to the area, without first proving that the area was economically unstable. Therefore, for eminent domain to apply in matters of urban rejuvenation, the area under consideration may be in good condition, but the state—or a private agent of the state—may determine that it is not good enough. There is no evidence offered by the respondent, or required by the Court, to prove that the area was blighted or that the economic plan would be effective.

> Alternatively, petitioners maintain that for takings of this kind we should require a "reasonable certainty" that the expected public benefits will actually accrue. Such a rule, however, would represent an even greater departure from our precedent. "When the legislature's purpose is legitimate and its means are not irrational, our cases make clear that empirical debates over the wisdom of takings—no less than debates over the wisdom of other kinds of socioeconomic legislation—are not to be carried out in the federal courts." . . . A constitutional rule that required postponement of the judicial approval of every condemnation until the likelihood of success of the plan had been assured would unquestionably impose a significant impediment to the successful consummation of many such plans. (*Kelo v. City of New London,* 2005, 125 S. Ct. at 2672–2673)

The problem with this reasoning that is never addressed by the Court, either in the majority or the dissent, is that there is no reason to have a requirement that a plan be well researched in order to pass constitutional muster if the results of that plan are never presented to the Court. How does the Court know, other than a timeline provided by the respondents, that the plan was legitimate?

Because the redevelopment plan was "comprehensive" and it took a long time to create, the Court determined that it was legitimate. The logic, I assume, since at no point does Stevens spell it out, is that because the plan was comprehensive and made after a deliberative process, the plan meets the requirements of due process, which then makes the seizure legitimate on Fourteenth Amendment grounds as well as Fifth. But because Stevens never says why a comprehensive and deliberative plan makes a difference, my analysis may be erroneous. The second option is that Stevens reasoned that if the plan was well thought out that the Court would be justified in deferring to the state. Whereas had the plan been an overnight development with no evidence of research, then the Court would be able to review the decision of the state as the state would not have possessed the necessary information and expertise. But if this logic is what Stevens had intended, it is obviously inconsistent with other parts of his decision.

There is yet a third option in trying to unravel the unexplained logic of Stevens. For Stevens, as for the petitioners, there was a concern that the property seizure was done by a private entity for the benefit of a private entity and not the public good. But with stunning certainty, Stevens suggests that because the plan was well thought out, there is no risk of this occurring:

> Nor would the City be allowed to take property under the mere pretext of a public purpose, when its actual purpose was to bestow a private benefit. The takings before us, however, would be executed pursuant to a "carefully considered" development plan. The trial judge and all the members of the Supreme Court of Connecticut agreed that there was no evidence of an illegitimate purpose in this case. Therefore, as was true of the statute challenged in *Midkiff*, the City's development plan was not adopted "to benefit a particular class of identifiable individuals." (*Kelo v. City of New London,* 2005, 125 S. Ct. at 2662)

Why his certainty on this point seems stunning is that earlier in the opinion Stevens acknowledges that, "The NLDC intended the development plan to capitalize on the arrival of the Pfizer facility and the new commerce it was expected to attract" (*Kelo v. City of New London,* 2005, 125 S. Ct. at 2658–2659). There is no inquiry into the level of involvement Pfizer had in the redevelopment plan. While it is unlikely that Pfizer had a direct role in the NLDC's plan, it is certainly worthy of consideration in order to understand if property was being seized for private benefit alone. The Court writes, "Such a one-to-one transfer of property, executed outside the confines of an integrated development plan, is not presented in this case" (*Kelo v. City of New London,* 2005, 125 S. Ct. at 2667). But even if Pfizer was not present in the NLDC deliberation, the fact that there was a one-to-one transfer of property is not avoided given that private property was seized by a private company and turned over to private developers. Stevens does not satisfactorily address the issue that the government, or another public agency, was not going to develop the land, but the land was going to be turned over to private companies who would profit from the development of the land. Nor is the fact that the NLDC was not a government agency given much attention. The fact that a city government can develop a private entity and bestow upon it the power of eminent domain seems striking and worthy of lengthy consideration. But the Court felt otherwise.

Partly because there was a "carefully considered development plan," the Court rejected the petitioners' request for a bright-line rule restricting economic benefit as grounds for establishing the public good. The petitioners were concerned that absent such a rule there would be no protection against government transfers of private property for private benefit.

Putting aside the unpersuasive suggestion that the City's plan will provide
only purely economic benefits . . . There is, moreover, no principled way of
distinguishing economic development from the other public purposes that we
have recognized. In our cases upholding takings that facilitated agriculture and
mining, for example, we emphasized the importance of those industries to the
welfare of the States in question . . . we endorsed the purpose of transforming
a blighted area into a "well-balanced" community through redevelopment. . . .
Clearly, there is no basis for exempting economic development from our traditionally broad understanding of public purpose. (*Kelo v. City of New London*,
2005, 125 S. Ct. at 2665–2667)

The discussion of whether economic benefit ought to be considered a
public good occurs in greater detail later in this chapter, but what can be said
now is that Stevens's characterization of Fort Trumbull as a blighted area,
by his own earlier admission (*Kelo v. City of New London*, 2005, 125 S. Ct.
at 2661), is factually inaccurate. Moreover, Stevens's historical reference to
the Mill Acts in support of his position is historically inaccurate. The Mill
Acts, which were extended to the mining industry, determined that certain
industries must be able to operate for the community to exist. Thus, the
public good in these cases is defined as the existence of the community,
not the economic improvement of the community (Gold 2007, p. 101,
103–105; Epstein 1985, p. 170–172, 173–176). Therefore, the ground on
which he builds his conclusion that economic benefit is a public good is
weak, and will grow weaker when the founding generation's understanding
of public use and public good developed in earlier chapters is revisited later
in this chapter.

Even if Stevens is correct in claiming that "the government's pursuit of the
public purpose will often benefit individual private parties" (*Kelo v. City of
New London*, 2005, 125 S. Ct. at 2666), he does not get around the public use
problem because his definition of the public use is too broad:

[T]his is not a case in which the City is planning to open the condemned
land—at least not in its entirety—to use by the general public. Nor will the
private lessees of the land in any sense be required to operate like common
carriers, making their services available to all comers. But although such a
projected use would be sufficient to satisfy the public use requirement, this
"Court long ago rejected any literal requirement that condemned property be
put into use for the general public." Indeed, while many state courts in the
mid-19th century endorsed "use by the public" as the proper definition of
public use, that narrow view steadily eroded over time. Not only was the "use
by the public" test difficult to administer . . . but it proved to be impractical
given the diverse and always evolving needs of society. (*Kelo v. City of New
London*, 2005, 125 S. Ct. at 2663)

Stevens had created a problem for himself. Even though he earlier established that the needs of society and how to serve them are best determined by legislators and other government agents (*Kelo v. City of New London,* 2005, 125 S. Ct. at 2663–2664, 2665, 2668), he has now determined that the Court's definition of what constitutes a public use has changed because of the evolving needs of society. The Supreme Court is the only authority cited by Stevens that thinks the public use standard is too narrow to serve the needs of society. It is unclear, if not impossible, to determine why Stevens thinks that the needs of society cannot be determined by the Court in one instance but can be in another. Therefore, he has made his decision according to the Court's conception of the public use while at same time admitting that the Court is not qualified to determine what that is. The majority opinion fails to remain consistent on this point.

Building on this introduction to the case, I will now provide a more detailed critique of the Court's decision by focusing on its understanding of public use, public good, and its refusal to apply the Bill of Rights to the states.

III B. A Critique of the Court's Use of Public Use, Public Good, and Failure to Incorporate the Fifth

There is no shortage of definitions offered by property rights advocates on the meaning of public use. As Thomas Cooley explains, "public use implies a possession, occupation, and enjoyment of the land by the public or public agencies. . . ." (Cooley 1868, p. 531). Richard Epstein has grounded his definition of public use in his reading of Locke, which leads him to the conclusion that "the public use requirement should ensure the 'fair' allocation of surplus by preventing any group from appropriating more than a pro rata share" (Epstein 1985, p. 164). While I may agree to some degree with each of these statements, neither goes very far in convincing those who do not already share their views, nor in justifying their own position within the American context. Attempts to define the public use in the American context must begin with a normative defense of private property. But explaining why property is good, or what it is good for, does not go very far in persuading those who think that, as Justice Stevens does, such normative determinations are best left in the hands of legislators. Critiques of the Court's treatment of property must begin, and perhaps end, with normative considerations, but to complete the argument one must provide a discussion of how the Court has departed from the intention of the framers and ratifiers of the Bill of Rights. Up to now, I have traced property rights from the common law to the Fifth Amendment; now I will show how the Court has departed from the earlier tradition and redefined property rights, beginning with the Court's interpretation of public use.

In *Kelo*, primarily citing *Fallbrook Irrigation District v. Bradley*[10] and *Berman v. Parker*,[11] the Court adopted the now standard definition of public use as public purpose. What is not made clear by the Court, at any point, is why the original wording of the Constitution is not good enough, or less useful than the Court's choice of words. Why does the Court think that its substitution of one word for another provides any more certainty, or is anymore constitutional, than the original wording of the Constitution? It seems obvious that interpreting public use as public purpose is a conscious departure from the literal wording of the document. Even those who do not buy into the original meaning method of constitutional interpretation must admit that substituting one word for another constitutes a redefinition. If words are to mean anything, then they cannot be changed without also changing the meaning. If the framers and ratifiers of the Fifth Amendment had meant public purpose, then it stands to reason they would have used that word, unless of course one were to assume that these men had a more limited vocabulary than we do. Moreover, there is no historical evidence to support this reading of the phrase. Redefining the public use requirement by substituting use with purpose is simply a maneuver, with no constitutional or historical justification, which the Court employed to resolve a difficult legal matter. The changing definition of public use reflects the Court's willingness to allow property seizures that would otherwise be found unconstitutional. Proponents of the Court's decision in the recent property rights cases have accused the Court's critics of calling for a *Lochner*-era jurisprudence in which there is a presumption of liberty rather than a presumption of constitutionality (Burke 2006, p. 703). Suffice it to say, the two are not exclusive, and had the Court not changed the original language of the Constitution, the presumption of both constitutionality and liberty could have been preserved.

Early in the Court's history it decided that there is no instance "in which a legislative act to transfer property of A to B without his consent has ever been held a constitutional exercise of legislative power in any state in the union" (*Wilkinson v Leland*, 1829, 27 U.S. 658). Justice Stevens chooses to depart from this decision, even when citing it as an authority. Justice Stevens suggests that there will be some private gain in all acts for the public good, and an act cannot be found to run against the public good simply because some benefit more than others. While Richard Epstein may disagree, this logic seems to have some constitutional justification. But, what Stevens lacks in support of his argument are facts. In both *Kelo* and *Berman*, property was transferred from one private owner to another without the first owner's consent through a legislative act, thus making it more than just an ancillary private benefit that resulted from pursuing the public good. Neither case provides a constitutional justification for its reading; rather the majority in each case based its reasoning on what was most practical at the time. The only way the Court could justify allowing private property transfers via eminent domain—or allow property seizures that would result in prohibiting public access to the end result—without owner consent was by expanding what it meant by public use. But, while citing an earlier case that the Court ignored, or violated the precedent of, serves some purpose, it does not provide a relevant critique of the current Court's position as it too is relying on precedent. That is, the source of one's criticism must come from some place other than the Court. But, since that was what I did in chapters 1 through 4, now it is time to show that the Court has departed from the original meaning and its own earlier definition of public use. Furthermore, I will provide an analysis of the case that shows the faulty reasoning used that expanded the definition of public use beyond its constitutional limits.

The public use requirement has not always been so lenient. In *Cole v. La Grange*,[12] the Court decided that the government could not issue bonds to a private enterprise to help finance the operation of a mill as that would constitute a private, not a public, use. In *Missouri Pacific Railway Company v. Nebraska*,[13] the taking of private property for the private use of another was determined to be a violation of due process. The city of Cincinnati fell to the Court's strict interpretation of the public use requirement when in the *City of Cincinnati v. Vester*,[14] the Court decided that when the city confiscated too much land for a road project and sold the unused seized land to a private owner, the city had violated the public use requirement. In the hands of the Court, this reading of the public use requirement—while it saw some variation before—changed dramatically in the New Deal era. In *United States ex rel. Tennessee Valley Authority v. Welch*,[15] the Court deferred to the legislature's determination of public use when it upheld the action of the Tennessee Valley Authority that resulted in the flooding of private property as part of a flood control program. Such deference to legislative authority would require the Court to expand the definition of public use. The majority in *Berman* was more than happy to oblige.

In the 1940s, Washington, D.C. had to figure out a way to deal with its growing slums and urban blight. Congress passed the District of Columbia Redevelopment Act of 1945 to help deal with the problem. The Act authorized the National Capital Planning Commission to develop comprehensive land use plans that would include the authorization of property seizures via eminent domain once the specific redevelopment plans had passed through a public hearing and gained the approval for the District of Columbia Redevelopment Land Agency. Once the land had been seized, government agencies would develop some of the land, and the remainder would be turned over to private businesses to develop.[16] As a result of this policy, Max Morris—and eventually his executors—brought suit as his department store, which was not in disrepair but had just undergone a renovation, was targeted for seizure and would be sold or leased to other private owners for redevelopment. Morris objected on the grounds that his property was being taken for private gain, not public use, and that his property was not contributing to the urban decline.

The Court pursued the same course of action we saw in *Kelo,* which was to defer to the legislative branch on the matters under consideration. Writing for a unanimous Court, Douglas wrote:

> We do not sit to determine whether a particular housing project is or is not desirable. The concept of the public welfare is broad and inclusive. . . . The values it represents are spiritual as well as physical, aesthetic as well as monetary. It is within the power of the legislature to determine that the community should be beautiful as well as healthy, spacious as well as clean, well-balanced as well as carefully patrolled. In the present case, the Congress and its authorized agencies have made determinations that take into account a wide variety of values. It is not for us to reappraise them. If those who govern the District of Columbia decide that the Nation's Capital should be beautiful as well as sanitary, there is nothing in the Fifth Amendment that stands in the way. . . . Subject to specific constitutional limitations, when the legislature has spoken, the public interest has been declared in terms well-nigh conclusive. In such cases the legislature, not the judiciary, is the main guardian of the public needs to be served by social legislation, whether it be Congress legislating concerning the District of Columbia or the States legislating concerning local affairs. (*Berman v. Parker,* 1954, 348 U.S. at 33)

There is no problem in concluding that Congress is better equipped than the Court to determine what the public needs and how to get it. The problem comes when the Court does not subject Congress to "specific constitutional limitations" and allows it to act with carte blanche. The same reasoning is used in *Kelo* and therefore leads to the same problem discussed earlier, which is, this allows the government to use eminent domain to transfer property from one private owner to another:

> Once the object is within the authority of Congress, the means by which it will be attained is also for Congress to determine. Here one of the means chosen is the use of private enterprise for redevelopment of the area. Appellants argue that this makes the project a taking from one businessman for the benefit of another businessman. But the means of executing the project are for Congress and Congress alone to determine, once the public purpose has been established. (*Berman v. Parker,* 1954, 348 U.S. at 34)

Therefore, without addressing it, the *Berman* Court overturned *Wilkinson v. Leland*, in which the Court determined that in no instance could this sort of transfer be found constitutional, and *Olcott v. The Supervisors* in which the Court wrote, "the right of eminent domain nowhere justifies taking property for a private use" (*Olcott v. The Supervisors,* 1872, 83 U.S. 694).

Of course, these conclusions could not have been reached without redefining the public use requirement. Public use became public purpose, and public use is to be determined by the legislature alone. But, one might be able to go even further and conclude that even public purpose is not required to make a taking legitimate only that, in the Court's view, one is compensated for the taking. The second to last sentence of the *Berman* decision reads, "The rights of these property owners are satisfied when they receive that just compensation which the Fifth Amendment exacts as the price of the taking." Therefore, the only Fifth Amendment requirement to make a taking constitutional is just compensation (Vance 2007, p. 27). Public use disappears as a requirement. The Court in *Kelo,* and in *Berman,* decided that to require a development to be a direct public benefit, or require public access, in order to meet the public use requirement was too restrictive of a standard, and that anything that may confer a benefit upon the public, as determined through legislation, meets the Fifth Amendment requirement. But, the Court lacks a foundation for its rewording of the Constitution. "The case, however, does not fall under the first two heads of public use: no pure public good is provided, nor is there any universal right of access to the plaintiff's property after the conveyance. In the end, therefore, community redevelopment plans rest on the necessity argument" (Epstein 1985, p. 179). The Court, in *Fallbrook, Berman*, and *Kelo,* merely cite precedent or the demands of the public without consulting the Constitution or searching for its original meaning.

Even if one agrees with the reasoning of *Berman,* despite the lack of constitutional and historical support, one has to recognize that *Berman* is not directly applicable to *Kelo* for the simple reason that in *Kelo* there is no blighted area. In *Berman,* legislation was passed because the area was blighted; in *Kelo,* neither side claimed that the area to be redeveloped was blighted. Therefore, if one chooses to be generous to the *Berman* Court, it can be said that in *Berman* the need for government action was necessary as the condition of the city was such that it was no longer safe or healthy.[17] That is, the city could no longer provide those things to its citizens that are required for a government to provide its citizens in order to maintain its legitimacy as a governing body.

> Miserable and disreputable housing conditions may do more than spread disease and crime and immorality. They may also suffocate the spirit by reducing the

people who live there to the status of cattle. They may indeed make living an almost insufferable burden. They may also be an ugly sore, a blight on the community which robs it of charm, which makes it a place from which men turn. The misery of housing may despoil a community as an open sewer may ruin a river. (*Berman v. Parker,* 1954, 348 U.S. at 32–33)

Such a standard was not upheld in *Kelo* as such a condition was not present. There was no threat to health or safety in New London, CT, as there was in Washington, D.C. The *Kelo* Court did not even follow precedent; they expanded the definition of what constitutes a public purpose.

The discussion of public use requires a discussion of the Court's understanding of the public good, as the determination of the public good has been determined to be in the hands of lawmakers, and the public use is satisfied so long as the public good is sought. While it has been shown that the Court does not ground its redefinition of public use in much more than judicial fiat, a discussion of its definition of the public good will show just how far the *Kelo* Court departed from the original meaning of the Constitution, specifically from the public use requirement. By expanding the definition of public use, the Court risks neglecting the public good, as it is the public use requirement, along with just compensation, that ensures that the public good is achieved and not the good of some citizens at the expense of others. "The Fifth Amendment's guarantee that private property shall not be taken for a public use without just compensation was designed to bar Government from forcing some people alone to bear public burdens which, in all fairness and justice, should be borne by the public as a whole" (*Armstrong v. United States,* 1795, 28 F. Cas. at 1012).

In *Carolene Products,*[18] the New Deal Court ushered in a new era of defining the public good by showing greater deference to the legislature in applying a minimal scrutiny standard to economic regulation questions. But, deferring to the legislative branch does not mean the Court must relinquish its ability to determine what is constitutional or whether the legislative branch has violated those rights the Constitution is designed to protect. In addition to the examples cited earlier, Justice Samuel Chase makes this point clear in *Calder v. Bull*[19] when he writes:

The people of the United States erected their constitutions, or forms of government, to establish justice, to promote the general welfare, to secure the blessings of liberty, and to protect their persons and property from violence. The purposes for which men enter into society will determine the nature and terms of the social compact, and as they are the foundation of the legislative power, they will decide what are the proper objects of it. The nature and ends of legislative power will limit the exercise of it. This fundamental principle flows from the very nature of our free republican governments that no man should be compelled to do what the laws do not require nor to refrain from acts which the laws permit. There are acts which the federal or state legislature cannot do without exceeding their authority. There are certain vital principles in our free republican governments which will determine and overrule an apparent and flagrant abuse of legislative power, as to authorize manifest injustice by positive law or to take away that security for personal liberty or private property for the protection whereof the government was established. An act of the legislature (for I cannot call it a law) contrary to the great first principles of the social compact cannot be considered a rightful exercise of legislative authority. The obligation of a law in governments established on express compact and on republican principles must be determined by the nature of the power on which it is founded. (*Calder v. Bull,* 1798, 3 U.S. (3 Dall.) at 388)

Justice Chase clearly reflects Locke's understanding of the social contract as well as those of the founders who adopted Locke's position. But, Chase does not leave it for us to imagine what he might have said with regard to transfers of private property between individuals via eminent domain, as he makes the same point that would be made nearly thirty years later in *Wilkinson v. Leland:*

A few instances will suffice to explain what I mean. A law that punished a citizen for an innocent action, or in other words for an act which when done was in violation of no existing law; a law that destroys or impairs the lawful private contracts of citizens; a law that makes a man a judge in his own cause; or a law that takes property from A and gives it to B. It is against all reason and justice for a people to entrust a legislature with such powers, and therefore it cannot be presumed that it has done it. (*Calder v. Bull,* 1798, 3 U.S. (3 Dall.) at 388)

In addition to a profound defense of property rights, Justice Chase shows again that, in the early republic, procedural due process (instrumental) rights and property (intrinsic) rights are deemed consistent with one another. They were not considered, as they are today, along different ideological dimensions.

While it is established that the jurists in the early republic were in support of property rights, and in overturning a legislative act when it conflicted with a higher law, it is not yet understood where they might have stood on the public good and its relationship to property. It is reasonable to assume that they had the same view as those who drafted and ratified the constitutions and amendments on which they based their decisions, but such an assumption is unnecessary as they have spoken in their own voice on the matter. Justice Paterson in *Vanhorne's Lessee v. Dorrance*[20] wrote, "It is difficult to form a case, in which the necessity of a state can be of such a nature, as to authorize or excuse the seizing of landed property belonging to one citizen, and giving it to another citizen" (*Vanhorne's Lessee v. Dorrance,* 1795, 2 U.S. (2 Dall.) at 311). The Courts of *Berman, Kelo,* and in *Hawaii Housing Authority v. Midkiff* argued that even a transfer of property from one citizen to another was justified so long as it served the public good, which would then make such a transfer for the public use. Recent cases have established that so long as there is a potential public benefit that transferring property that creates a direct private benefit is constitutional.

But, the departure does not end here. As shown in the discussion of the founding documents, the only occasion in which property could be seized was when the existence of the community depended upon it and there was a real and direct public benefit. Justice Paterson's opinion in *Vanhorne's Lessee* shows that a position close to my own was adopted by the early Court:

> The Constitution encircles, and renders it a holy thing. We must, gentlemen, bear constantly in mind, that the present is a case of landed property; vested by law in one set of citizens, attempted to be divested, for the purpose of vesting the same property in another set of citizens. It cannot be assimilated to the case of personal property taken or used in time of war or famine, or other extreme necessity; it cannot be assimilated to the temporary possession of land itself, on a pressing public emergency, or the spur of the occasion. (*Vanhorne's Lessee v. Dorrance,* 1795, 2 U.S. (2 Dall.) at 311)

It might be argued that in *Berman* there was a real emergency. But neither in *Midkiff* nor in *Kelo* is that argument made, nor could it plausibly be made in either of those cases.

To reduce the social and economic evils that resulted from the land oligopoly in Hawaii, whose origins were traceable to its former system based upon economic principles of feudalism, the Hawaii legislature passed the Land Reform Act of 1967 that authorized the Hawaii Housing Authority to condemn tracts of land that it would then seize and compensate the owners for their loss, and resell the tracts to the private landowners who had been leasing the land prior to the condemnation. Frank Midkiff and the Hawaii Housing Authority could not come to an agreement on the purchase of his land, so he brought suit in district court to challenge the constitutionality of the act under the Takings Clause. When the Court heard *Hawaii Housing Authority v. Midkiff,*[21] it rejected Midkiff's claim. In assessing whether the taking was a public use, the Court also considered the proper definition of the public good. Their first approach to defining public use was to rely on *Berman.* The Court held that for the same reasons expressed in *Berman,* this seizure constituted a public use, and therefore taking property from one individual and giving it to another is a valid use of the state's police powers (*Hawaii Housing Authority v. Midkiff,* 1984, 467

U.S. at 39–244). The Court, like it had been in *Berman,* was highly deferential to the legislative authority to define public use and decide the manner in which it was to be pursued "unless the use be palpably without reasonable foundation" (*Hawaii Housing Authority v. Midkiff,* 1984, 467 U.S. at 241). However, the Court does not provide a definition of "reasonable foundation."

There is a two-pronged test that the Court invokes in *Midkiff,* which is also adopted in *Berman* and *Kelo.* The legislature's purpose must be legitimate, and the means for pursuing that purpose must not be irrational (*Hawaii Housing Authority v. Midkiff,* 1984, 467 U.S. at 242–243).

In all three cases, the Court defers to the legislature's choice of method and for nearly identical reasons. But on the first prong of the test, the Court decides in *Midkiff* that it must define public good in order to define public use, as the public good requirement must be met in order to determine whether the purpose is legitimate (*Hawaii Housing Authority v. Midkiff,* 1984, 467 U.S. at 241). The Court decided that to reduce the effects of a land oligopoly with origins traceable to a former political regime, thereby opening the avenues to landownership to more people, is consistent with the intentions of the settlers of the original American colonies (*Hawaii Housing Authority v. Midkiff,* 1984, 467 U.S. at 241). Therefore, the public good was achieved through the Land Reform Act of 1967 because inequality in land distribution was reduced. In other words, because land was being taken from people who had a lot of it, and being redistributed—through sale or lease—to people who did not have it, by way of eminent domain, the public good was achieved. The Court suggests that using eminent domain to transfer property from one private owner to another for the purpose of advancing equality and balancing the marketplace is justifiable because it is for the public good (*Hawaii Housing Authority v. Midkiff,* 1984, 467 U.S. at 243–244). The Court does this while citing cases that have stated that "one person's property may not be taken for the benefit of another private person without a justifying public purpose, even though compensation be paid" (*Hawaii Housing Authority v. Midkiff,* 1984, 467 U.S. at 241). The Court seems to think that it sidesteps this problem by defending the seizure in question as a public purpose. But just because there is a public purpose does not make it a public good, nor does it mean it provides a public use, at least in the most strict sense.

There are at least three problems with the Court's reasoning that the pursuit of equality in land distribution is consistent with the public good and therefore a legitimate employment of the Takings Clause to achieve that end. First, to say that the purpose of the original settlers was to ensure protection against a land oligopoly linked to title is to misread history. As demonstrated throughout chapter 3, the settlers designed their constitutions to protect an individual's right to own land. At no point in any of the original charters or constitutions was there a prohibition against a land oligopoly or a provision for an equal distribution of land ownership. While they may have been escaping the old world rules of land ownership and title, they still protected rules of inheritance,[22] which indicates that the passing down of land through generations—which naturally leads to disproportionate levels of land ownership—was a protected right and the preferred policy position of the early settlers, thus rendering O'Connor's argument inaccurate. Second, based on the evidence provided in chapters 3 and 4, there is no reason to believe that the ratifiers of the Constitution and the Fifth Amendment would have been in favor of eminent domain being used for the purpose of establishing economic equality. It seems unlikely that those in the founding generation—such as John Adams, who wrote, "The moment the idea is admitted into society that property is not as sacred as the laws of God . . . anarchy and tyranny commence," or Thomas Jefferson, who wrote, "The free exercise of association is the guarantee to every one of a free exercise of his industry, and the fruits acquired by it," and particularly Madison who argued in *Federalist* #10 that while a diversity of the faculties of men gives rise to an unequal distribution of property, the protection of property, and the faculties from which they are derived, must be the first object of government—would have approved of government-imposed economic equality through property seizures. Third, the Court states that homeownership is preferable to leasing the land one lives on, which is why ending the oligopoly is beneficial, as it allows for a greater number of homeowners, and homeownership is a positive (*Hawaii Housing Authority v. Midkiff*, 1984, 467 U.S. at 242). But this statement is contradictory. The Court is saying that in order to bestow the benefits of homeownership upon those who do not enjoy the benefit, the state of Hawaii must limit these benefits to others. To simplify: To protect one's access to property and property rights, the government must take property away from others, thus limiting the property rights of this second group. The means defy the ends.[23]

Midkiff helps us understand the Court's reasoning in *Kelo* in that the *Kelo* Court justifies its broad interpretation of public use partly by relying on *Midkiff*'s definition of the public good. *Midkiff* raises different considerations than does *Berman,* as the focus in *Midkiff* was on how the public good is defined via public use, rather than focusing on public use in isolation. The Court, by relying on *Midkiff*, defined the taking in *Kelo* as a public good, thus meeting the public use requirement.

The question remains as to what standard ought to be adopted to measure the public good. As already stated with reference to public use, the standard that ought to be adopted is that which the ratifiers of the Constitution and the Fifth Amendment adopted for themselves. This method is valid only if no amendment has been passed to revise the Fifth Amendment's Taking

Clause, which there has not been, and if we use the Constitution as the measure by which we determine the justness of a particular policy, which we presumably do. As demonstrated in chapter 4, property may be seized when the public use is real and direct and when the public good granted by the seizure is demonstrably greater than it would have been had no seizure taken place. The only time, according to the founder's view, that the public good is achieved by a seizure is when a property seizure allows the government to serve its role as a protector of rights. Therefore, if not seizing property will cause the government to lose its ability to carry out its function of "protecting the diversity of faculties of men," then the seizure would achieve the public good. People form a government to protect their inalienable rights, which are under constant threat when government is absent. Government allows people to enjoy their rights, and government then becomes illegitimate once it becomes a threat to those rights it was instituted to protect. This is a Lockean view of government to be sure (Chapter XIX; particularly § 222), but it is the founders' as well, as seen in chapters 3 and 4. There are a few passages not cited in the earlier chapters that elucidate this point:

> That government is, or ought to be, instituted for the common benefit, protection and security of the people, nation or community; and not for the particular emolument or advantage of any single man, family, or set of men, who are a part only of that community; And that the community hath an indubitable, unalienable, and indefeasible right to reform, alter, or abolish government in such manner as shall be by that community judged most conducive to the public weal. (Pennsylvania Declaration of Rights, 1776, Section 5, p. 265)
>
> That all power being originally inherent in, and consequently, derived from, the people; therefore, all officers of government, whether legislative or executive, and their trustees and servants, and at all time accountable to them. (Vermont Declaration of Rights, 1777, Section 5, p. 323; section 6 repeats verbatim section 5 of the Pennsylvania Declaration)[24]
>
> All men are born equally free and independent; therefore, all government of right originates from the people, is founded in consent, and instituted for the general good (Section 1). . . . All men have certain natural, essential, and inherent rights; among which are—the enjoying and defending of life and liberty— acquiring, possessing, and protecting property—and in a word, of seeking and obtaining happiness (Section 2). . . . When men enter into a state of society, they surrender up some of their natural rights to that society, in order to insure the protection of others; and without such an equivalent, the surrender is void (Section 3). . . . (New Hampshire Bill of Rights, 1783, p. 375; section 10 of this document repeats section 5 of Pennsylvania's Declaration as well)

Despite the criticism already levied against the Court and its misapplication of the Constitution's requirement of public use and public good, there is still another—one that has not before been raised in the literature. In leaving it up to the states whether they will follow Connecticut's lead or offer greater protection to property owners requires the Court to assume that the Fifth Amendment offers only a minimal protection of property rights:

> We emphasize that nothing in our opinion precludes any State from placing further restrictions on its exercise of the takings power. Indeed, many States already impose "public use" requirements that are stricter than the federal baseline. Some of these requirements have been established as a matter of state constitutional law, while others are expressed in state eminent domain statutes that carefully limit the grounds upon which takings may be exercised. As the submissions of the parties and their amici make clear, the necessity and wisdom of using eminent domain to promote economic development are certainly matters of legitimate public debate. This Court's authority, however, extends only to determining whether the City's proposed condemnations are for a "public use" within the meaning of the Fifth Amendment to the Federal Constitution. Because over a century of our case law interpreting that provision dictates an affirmative answer to that question, we may not grant petitioners the relief that they seek. (*Kelo v. City of New London*, 2005, 125 S. Ct. at 2666)

I have shown this reading of the Fifth Amendment to be inconsistent with the intent of those who drafted and ratified the Bill of Rights. But, the Court has told the states that its reading of the Fifth Amendment is not binding on the states. This aspect of the Court's decision violates the practice of incorporation by which the Court has extended the protections offered by the Bill of Rights to the states. While proponents of the New Federalism doctrine might see this as a victory, particularly those who think that the Court's reading of the Fourteenth Amendment is too expansive (Vance 2007), it is a hollow one. Oddly enough, those who traditionally come to the defense of the incorporation doctrine are generally those who criticize those who seek greater protection of property rights (Burke 2006); and those who seek greater protection for property rights can be more often found opposing the Court's use of the Fourteenth Amendment to incorporate the Bill of Rights. My reading of the incorporation doctrine as it applies to *Kelo* will appeal to both sides—or perhaps alienate both—by showing that the incorporation of the Takings Clause via the Fourteenth Amendment is consistent with the intentions of the ratifiers of the Fifth and Fourteenth Amendments.[25]

The question of whether the states were bound by the Bill of Rights was sufficiently answered by the Supreme Court in *Barrron v. Baltimore*.[26] In this case, John Barron and John Craig sued the city of Baltimore for $20,000 in damages that were incurred as a result of the city's construction project that interfered with Barron and Craig's business. Chief Justice John Marshall, writing for a unanimous Court, declared that the Bill of Rights applied to the federal government only, and not to the states:

> The Constitution was ordained and established by the people of the United States for themselves, for their own government, and not for the government of the individual States. Each State established a constitution for itself, and in that constitution provided such limitations and restrictions on the powers of its particular government as its judgment dictated. The people of the United States framed such a government for the United States as they supposed best adapted to their situation and best calculated to promote their interests. The powers they conferred on this government were to be exercised by itself, and the limitations on power, if expressed in general terms, are naturally, and we think necessarily, applicable to the government created by the instrument. They are limitations of power granted in the instrument itself, not of distinct governments framed by different persons and for different purposes. (*Barron v. Baltimore,* 1833, 32 U.S. (7 Pet.) at 247)

The result of this particular case was unfortunate for Barron and Craig, but it cannot be said to be faulty in its constitutional reasoning, even though Marshall inadequately addressed the plaintiff's argument that the Tenth Amendment made the Fifth applicable to the states. In any event, when Marshall made his decision in *Barron,* there was little risk, or so he thought, of the states taking away the rights of its citizens given that the rights codified in the Bill of Rights already had been codified in the constitutions of the states and had been recommended by the states to the federal government for adoption.

Barron was decided prior to the ratification of the Fourteenth Amendment, which states in Section 1 that

> All persons born or naturalized in the United States and subject to the jurisdiction thereof are citizens of the United States and of the State wherein they reside. No State shall make or enforce any law which shall abridge the privileges or immunities of citizens of the United States; nor shall any State deprive any person of life, liberty, or property without due process of law; nor deny to any person within its jurisdiction the equal protection of the laws.

The question quickly arose as to whether this amendment, specifically this section which embodies the privileges or immunities clause and the due process clause, extended the Bill of Rights to the states. If so, then future decisions overturning *Barron's* refusal to extend the Bill of Rights to the states would be on safe constitutional ground even if one were to assume that Marshall's reasoning was constitutionally sound, because an amendment to the Constitution changes the document's meaning. Therefore, with regard to the Bill of Rights, the Constitution that Marshall read would have been different than the one read by those after the Fourteenth was ratified. But, extending the protections of the Bill of Rights to the states, known as *incorporation,* was not immediate. The Court decided in the *Slaughter-house Cases* that the privileges or immunities clause did not incorporate the Bill of Rights nor did the due process clause as decided in *Hurtado v. California.*[27]

But, soon after *Hurtado,* the Court changed its stance with regard to the due process clause while leaving the *Slaughterhouse* doctrine nearly untouched until recently in *Saenz v. Roe*[28] in which it has altered its use of the privileges or immunities clause. In 1897, the Court officially adopted the incorporation doctrine in a case dealing with an uncompensated taking. *Chicago, Burlington & Quincy v. Chicago*[29] resolved the question of whether the city of Chicago owed a railroad company a just compensation for the property the city seized under eminent domain. Rather than using *Barron* as a precedent, Justice Marshall Harlan, writing for the majority, extended Fifth Amendment protections to the states by employing the same argument that appeared in his *Hurtado* dissent:

If compensation for private property taken for public use is an essential element of due process of law as ordained by the Fourteenth Amendment, then the final judgment of a state court, under the authority of which the property is in fact taken, is to be deemed the act of the State within the meaning of that amendment. It is proper now to inquire whether the due process of law enjoined by the Fourteenth Amendment requires compensation to be made or adequately secured to the owner of private property taken for public use under the authority of a State (166 U.S. at 235). . . . Due protection of the rights of property has been regarded as a vital principle of republican institutions (166 U.S. at 235–236). . . . But if, as this court has adjudged, a legislative enactment, assuming arbitrarily to take the property of one individual and give it to another individual, would not be due process of law, as enjoined by the Fourteenth Amendment, it must be that the requirement of due process of law in that amendment is applicable to the direct appropriation by the State to public use, and without compensation, of the private property of the citizen (166 U.S. at 236). . . . "Whatever may have been the power of the States on this subject prior to the adoption of the Fourteenth Amendment to the Constitution, it seems clear that, since that amendment went into effect, such limitations and restraints have been placed upon their power in dealing with individual rights that the States cannot now lawfully appropriate private property for the public benefit or to public uses without compensation to the owner, and that any attempt so to do, whether done in pursuance of a constitutional provision or legislative enactment, whether done by the legislature itself or under delegated authority by one of the subordinate agencies of the State, and whether done directly, by taking the property of one person and vesting it in another or the public, or indirectly, through the forms of law, by appropriating the property and requiring the owner thereof to compensate himself, or to refund to another the compensation to which he is entitled, would be wanting in that 'due process of law' required by said amendment. The conclusion of the court on this question is that, since the adoption of the Fourteenth Amendment, compensation for private property taken for public uses constitutes an essential element in 'due process of law,' and that, without such compensation, the appropriation of private property to public uses, no matter under what form of procedure it is taken, would violate the provisions of the federal Constitution." (166 U.S. at 238–239; quoting Justice Jackson in *Scott v. Toledo*)

Justice Harlan made it clear that property rights are vital for preserving republican principles, and that the protection of property rights is ensured by the Fifth Amendment against action from any level or branch of government, via the due process clause of the Fourteenth Amendment. What is remarkable about this decision is that Justice Harlan had another outlet. The Constitution of Illinois, and various Illinois statutes and Chicago city ordinances consistent with the state constitution, provided the same protections as the Fifth Amendment. Justice Harlan chose to use the Fifth Amendment so he could press the incorporation doctrine, not because it was the only legal option on which he could base his opinion. The just compensation provision became the first provision of the Bill of Rights extended to the states. One could argue that *Barron* is more consistent with the vision of the founders, but one's attachment to the founders' intention must be tempered by the Fourteenth Amendment as the founders recognized that a constitutional amendment would necessarily override any part of the Constitution to which it applied.

The important question now is whether the Fourteenth Amendment is adequate grounds for incorporating the Bill of Rights. There was no doubt that the Fourteenth Amendment applied to the states, the only question was what rights did it extend to them. John Bingham, a representative from Ohio, authored the second sentence of the Fourteenth Amendment. Prior to authoring that sentence, Bingham had made several public statements about the importance of private property and that the Fifth Amendment protects natural rights to all persons (Siegan 1997, p. 36–37). Bingham's speeches on behalf of the Fourteenth Amendment recognized the importance of property in the pursuit of liberty. His remarks reflect a general trend in the understanding of the nation as a result of the Civil War. There was no longer any question of citizenship now that the right to secession had been revoked, rather each citizen's first allegiance—from the point of view of the Constitution—was to his or her nation, and then to the state. By extension then, all rights granted to citizens by the Constitution and Bill of Rights were valid in all circumstances.

When the Fourteenth Amendment states "nor shall any State deprive any person of life, liberty, or property, without due process of law," the assumption is that those mechanisms that constituted due process of law in the Bill of Rights remain the same in the Fourteenth Amendment. Thus, when the ratifiers of the Fifth Amendment understood due process of law to mean that a taking must be for a public use and required just compensation, so too is the same standard of due process understood when reading the Fourteenth Amendment. By adopting the same language as the Bill of Rights, the Fourteenth Amendment signaled that the intention was to extend the same rights to the states (Sandefur 2006, p. 62). Because the ratifiers and architects of the Fourteenth understood the relationship between property and procedural due process rights in a similar manner as their Fifth Amendment counterparts, to conclude that the Fourteenth incorporates the Fifth is not a stretch (Siegan 1997, p. 36–37).

While my argument throughout has been that the Court violated the Fifth Amendment in *Kelo*, I have just extended a separate argument that one can accept, even if one rejects my earlier contention on the Court's misapplication of the public use and public good requirements. Because the Court left it to the states to decide for themselves, it violated the Fourteenth Amendment by allowing for variation in the state adaptation of a constitutional right. While it established a baseline that the states could not go below, the Court left it to the states to determine for themselves what the Fifth Amendment meant by *public use*. It does not matter that the states were allowed to offer more protection and not less; the matter in contention is that since the incorporation doctrine took effect there has been a uniform standard that all states had to conform to, and that was the Constitution. Under *Kelo,* the Takings Clause has no meaning, not only because the Court read the meaning out of it by substituting public purpose for public use, but because it said there is no one proper interpretation, but there can be as many as fifty. It is hard to make the argument that a clause left undefined, in addition to allowing the substitution of one word for another, has any enforceable meaning. By not making a determination on what the definitive reading ought to be, the Court left it more vulnerable for future mischief, as now there are fewer restrictions on how it can be read.

By allowing states to interpret for themselves what a particular part of the Constitution means, the Court has committed itself to an understanding of rights—in this case, property rights—that does not recognize them as unalienable or natural, but as things which may be defined and redefined according to the political disposition of an actor. In defining public use and public good, the Court opened itself up to a similar attack. The result is, as will be demonstrated in the next chapter, that the protection of rights depends on the strength and influence of interested political forces rather than the Constitution.

SUMMARY

To continue with the line of argument that has been carried through this entire book, property rights are not separate from other rights. Property rights are intertwined with these other rights as property rights stem from, and protect, liberty which is the foundation of all rights. As John Trenchard writes in *Cato's Letters:*

> All Men are animated by the Passion of acquiring and defending Property, because Property is the best Support of the Independency, so passionately described by all Men. Even Men the most dependent have it constantly in their Heads and their Wishes, to become independent one Time or other; and the Property which they are acquiring, or mean to acquire by that Dependency, is intended to bring them out of it, and to procure them an agreeable Independency. And as Happiness is the Effect of Independency, and Independency the Effect of Property; so certain Property is the Effect of Liberty alone, and can only be secured by the Laws of Liberty. . . . (Trenchard 1987, p. 585)

And certainly, it was not only activists and pamphleteers who felt this way. Prominent politicians and jurists made their position known. Justice William Paterson wrote that, "the right of acquiring and possessing property, and having it protected, is one of the natural, inherent, and unalienable rights of man. No man would become a member of a community, in which he could not enjoy the fruits of his honest labour and industry. The preservation of property then is a primary object of the social compact. . . ." (*Vanhorne's Lessee v. Dorrance,* 1795, 2 U.S. (2 Dall.) at 310). Justice Joseph Story, one of the preeminent jurists in American history, wrote, "One of the fundamental objects of every good government must be the due administration of justice; and how vain it would be to speak of such an administration, when all property is subject to the will or caprice of the legislature and the rulers" (Story 1833, p. 664). As has been shown in this chapter, the majority's position in the three property rights cases discussed, specifically *Kelo*, is in direct conflict with the pre–New Deal conception of property rights. Even though Fifth Amendment protections were not consistently extended to the states until after the ratification of the Fourteenth Amendment, property rights enjoyed greater protection than they currently do post–New Deal.

The New Deal approach, most clearly seen in footnote four of *Carolene Products*,[30] bestowed a second-class status on property rights as it found other rights more worthy of due process protections (Ely 2005a, 2005b). Given that due process protections are not limited in the number of rights they can protect, the Court's treatment is peculiar in more than just its misreading of the Constitution. "A key feature of New Deal Constitutionalism was a judicially fashioned dichotomy between the rights of property owners and other personal liberties" (Ely 2005a, p. 46). Chief Justice Rehnquist echoes this concern when he wrote in *Dolan*, "We see no reason why the Takings Clause of the Fifth Amendment, as much a part of the Bill of Rights as the First Amendment or the Fourth Amendment, should be relegated to the status of a poor relation" (*Dolan v. City of Tigard*, 1994, 512 U.S. at 392).

Some have suggested that "since the expansive industrial revolution-based definition of public use is unnecessary, outdated, and arguably unsupported, in order to protect the institution of private property, which is closely intertwined with one's personal rights," there needs to be a new standard by which the courts must engage the public use question specifically (Kotlyarevskaya 2006, p. 225–226). I hesitate to adopt this position, as it was new interpretative strategies that started the problem. I recommend going back to the Constitution as it was originally conceived. I do not support all of the tenets of originalism or textualism, but I do support the premise that the Constitution ought to be the star by which judges set their bearings. I do think that we can come to an accurate understanding of the founders' Constitution by considering all of the founding documents and reading those political theorists who influenced those documents. Certainly this will lead to varying interpretations still, but the boundaries within which the disagreement occurs will be much narrower. If the people, the courts, the states, and Congress decide that what was intended by the Constitution on a particular matter no longer suits our needs, there is always Article V. The Court, or any branch at any level, should not serve as an Article V surrogate.

By giving judges the authority to determine what rights are, rights have become mutable and politicized. The consequence is that liberty, as the foundation for rights, is threatened. Once government officials are given the authority to determine what rights are, through channels independent of the Constitution, and to define for themselves what the Constitution means without reference to founding era documents, what were once inalienable, become debatable. If the threat was coming only from the government that would be one thing, but the greatest threat exists in the fact that academics and average citizens do not recognize that there is a connection between all rights, and that one does not have to choose between justice, general welfare, and property. Liberals and conservatives have chosen particular sets of rights they find more valuable than others, thus pitting the two sides against one another and making a zero-sum game out of the conflict. Meaning, rights become competing quantities in which to promote one means sacrificing another. Procedural due process rights, and other civil rights, are not inimical to property rights; in fact, those rights gain their value by the extent to which they protect property, justice. and the general welfare. Those rights considered inalienable by the Declaration of Independence and those goals listed in the Preamble of the Constitution work in concert. To deprive citizens of one right will eventually deprive citizens of all rights.

NOTES

1. 125 S. Ct. 2074.
2. 125 S. Ct. 2491.
3. 125 S. Ct. 2655.
4. 447 U.S. 255 (1980).
5. The Court stated that o.ther grounds were "permanent physical invasion, deprivation of all economically viable use, violation of the *Penn Central* guidelines, or land use exactions that amount to a per se physical taking because not closely tied to the impact of the proposed development" (Ely 2005a, p. 51).
6. Joseph Heller is the author of *Catch-22*.
7. 473 U.S. 172 (1985).
8. What should not be lost in all this, though the accusations are not on irrefutable ground, is the role Pfizer—another private company—played. Pfizer was looking to build a facility in New London, particularly in the Fort Trumbull area. The accusation is that Pfizer told the NLDC and city officials that it would build its new facilities only if there was a redevelopment plan underway for the waterfront area. Pfizer worked along side the NLDC to develop the plans that would make the city attractive for those with incomes exceeding $150,000 per year (Ted Mann, "Pfizer's Fingerprints on Fort Trumbull Plan," *The Day*, October 16, 2005, as cited in Sandefur 2006, p. 97–98).
9. Particularly disheartening is the fact that Susette Kelo and her neighbors were informed that their houses would be seized the day before Thanksgiving.
10. 164 U.S. 112 (1896). *Fallbrook Irrigation District* was not a case of eminent domain. Its importance here is to show that the Court in *Kelo* did not go back to the Constitution and apply its language, rather it went to another case to justify its transformation of public use into public purpose. The fact that *Fallbrook* was a case not dealing with eminent domain is even more disheartening for those who prefer a more faithful reading of the Constitution and application of precedent.
11. 348 U.S. 26 (1954).
12. 113 U.S. 1 (1885).
13. 164 U.S. 403 (1896).
14. 281 U.S. 439 (1930).
15. 327 U.S. 546 (1946). It is a well-known that the New Deal era brought about changes within each branch of government in which the government involvement in the private sector became more prominent given the dire circumstances created by the Great Depression.
16. Oddly, the *Berman* court did not consider *City of Cincinnati v. Vester* to be a valid reference.

17. Also, in utilities and transportation cases, there are some private goods that also meet the public use requirement as access to those things is open to all (Kotlyarevskaya 2006, p. 213–215).

18. 304 U.S. 144 (1938).

19. 3 U.S. (3 Dall.) 386.

20. 2 U.S. 304 (1795).

21. 467 U.S. 229 (1984).

22. The colonial declarations and state constitutions and declarations that protected inheritance from excessive taxing, seizure, and redistribution included: Massachusetts Body of Liberties, 1641, Section 10; New York Charter of Libertyes and Priviledges, 1683, paragraph 25; Pennsylvania Charter of Privileges, 1701, Section 7; Virginia Declaration of Rights, 1776, Section 1; New Jersey Constitution, 1776, Section 17; Maryland Declaration of Rights, 1776, Section 24; Connecticut Declaration of Rights, 1776, Section 2; and Georgia Constitution, 1777, Article 51.

23. State governments seized the opportunity opened to them by *Berman*, and confirmed by *Midkiff*, to achieve economically desirable ends through government authorized property transfers between private owners via eminent domain. The city of Detroit sought to stimulate its economy—thus satisfying both the public use and public good requirements as understood by the Supreme Court in *Berman*, *Midkiff*, and *Kelo*—by seizing an area of town and turning it over to a car manufacturer. In *Poletown Neighborhood Council v. City of Detroit* (304 N.W.2d 455 (Mich. 1981)), the Michigan Supreme Court upheld the condemnation and transfer of private homes and businesses to the General Motors Corporation because it determined that the private economic development would lead to more jobs and an increased tax revenue, thus satisfying the public use and public good requirements. But in 2004, the Michigan Supreme Court overturned *Poletown* in *County of Wayne v. Hathcock* (684 N.W.2d 765 (Mich. 2004)) by determining that economic development did not satisfy the public use or public good requirements. Michigan is not an anomaly. From 1998–2003 there have been more than 10,000 cases of government officials using, or threatening the use of, eminent domain on behalf of private developers (Sandefur 2006, p. 96).

24. Section 7 of the Massachusetts Declaration of Rights, 1780, repeats the same point in near identical words as Section 5 of the Pennsylvania Declaration. The Massachusetts document places a greater emphasis on protection, safety, prosperity, and happiness.

25. I offer nothing by way of solace to those who argue that the ratification of the Fourteenth Amendment was a violation of Article V. At this point, I make the assumption that the Fourteenth Amendment is legitimate, as engaging in that debate would go too far afield of the intentions of this book.

26. 32 U.S. (7 Pet.) 243 (1833).

27. 110 U.S. 516 (1884).

28. 526 U.S. 489 (1999).

29. 166 U.S. 226 (1897).

30. 304 U.S. 144.

Chapter 6

State Reactions to *Kelo v. City of New London*

It is the rare political issue that puts the NAACP and the Goldwater Institute on the same side, but that is exactly what happened when Susette Kelo appealed her case to the United States Supreme Court. The question considered by the Court was whether eminent domain could be used to transfer property from one private owner to another for future economic development. Over forty *amicus* briefs were filed—more than 60 percent of those were for Kelo—by such wide-ranging interests as the Cato Institute, NAACP, AARP, and the American Farm Bureau Federation. In a 5–4 decision, the Court decided against Kelo. The decision set off a firestorm of debate in which opponents of the decision made their opinion known in congressional hearings and in less formal environments.

While the decision did open the possibility for infringement on individual property rights, a reading of the decision will find that the final determination of whether to transfer property from one private owner to another via eminent domain lies with the states. The Court decided to let the states decide for themselves if they would allow eminent domain to be used in this fashion. So the decision, while intriguing for constitutional historians and legal scholars, provides a relevant avenue of investigation for those interested in state politics in general and legislative voting behavior in particular.

Because states can decide for themselves whether to allow property transfers between private owners via eminent domain, or restrict such employment of eminent domain, researchers can examine legislative responsiveness to constituent demands on this issue. One advantage of using *Kelo* in this type of study is the high saliency it has among citizens, as Americans cited—at the time of the decision—private property rights as the current legal issue they were most concerned about (Harwood 2005).

Scholarship on the U.S. Congress has found that constituency opinion and the party affiliation of the congressional member has an impact on roll-call voting behavior (Snyder and Groseclose 2001; McCarty, Poole, and Rosenthal 2001; Levitt 1996). These effects vary depending upon the bill under consideration (Clark and McGuire 1996; Meernik 1995), institutional constraints (Grofman, Griffin, and Glazer 1991), interest group involvement (Kollman 1997; Smith 1995), and individual characteristics of the congressional member (Stratmann 2000). Research on state legislatures has found similar patterns, but party discipline and organized interests tend to have a greater and more consistent impact at the state level than they do at the national level (Burstein and Linton 2002; Wiggins, Hamm, and Bell 1992). This study takes a highly salient issue and finds that state legislatures will pass bills that conform to the preference of the dominant party in the legislature and the constituency within that particular state. This study finds that the states that took action to restrict the application of post-*Kelo* eminent domain were those states where the dominant party and the largest economic interests opposed the decision. The results suggest that there has been a politicization of rights that needs to be recognized in order to appreciate how far we have departed from the founding generation's understanding of rights in general and property rights in particular.

I. A BRIEF REVIEW OF PRIVATE PROPERTY PROTECTION IN AMERICA

The Magna Carta of 1215 set limitations on the King's authority to take land from his subjects in chapters 29, 38, and 52. Modern commentators count up to eighteen rights of land references in the 1215 Charter (Hogue 1986). In the 1225 version of the Great Charter, similar provisions were made, and in some instances strengthened property rights—chapters 9, 29, 30, and 39. Lord Coke—who according to Edward Corwin was "first on the ground in the colonies"—provides the most authoritative interpretation of chapter 29, the chapter which enumerates many of those rights we now consider due process rights, including the right to property (Coke 1974). Coke was not alone. William Blackstone—the second most cited thinker in America from 1760–1805 (Lutz 1984)—found similar property protections in the Magna Carta, just as Coke before him and Hogue after him. Blackstone respected Coke's legal reasoning, but was more attached to the idea of natural rights than Coke. Among men's natural rights, according to Blackstone, was the right to property, a right that the government could not impinge upon (Blackstone 1979). In the eyes of the common law, as founded in the Magna Carta and interpreted by Coke and Blackstone, property rights were fundamental in protecting citizens and subjects from tyrannical rule. The common law heritage, at least in terms of property rights, found a home in America as well.

The U.S. Constitution takes a positive view of property and, in the Fifth Amendment, insists that government ought not infringe upon it. In the famed *Federalist #10*, James Madison argues, "The diversity of the faculties of men, from which the rights of property originate, is not less an insuperable obstacle to a uniformity of interests. The protection of these faculties is the first object of government" (#10: p. 43). This statement draws on John Locke's chapter V of the *Second Treatise of Government.* The idea of protecting property rights was supported by most of the founding generation and is reflected in the U.S. Constitution, colonial charters, state constitutions, and state laws. As demonstrated in chapters 3 and 4, the ratifiers of the Bill of Rights obviously reflect Locke's and the common law's understanding of property, as the Fifth Amendment discusses property and due process along the same dimension.

The only point this section makes is that the idea of property is a deeply ingrained right that draws on this nation's common law heritage to provide the reader with a brief review of the five previous chapters. With a proper understanding of the historical context and philosophical origins, it should be no surprise that the *Kelo* decision drew so much attention.

II. REVISITING THE DECISION

The legal question in *Kelo* centered on an urban rejuvenation initiative in New London, Connecticut. The plan sought to build a hotel, new residences, stores, and recreational facilities. The New London Development Council (NLDC), a private organization, was given authorization by the New London City Council to seize real estate by eminent domain for this purpose. Some of the seized land would be turned over to private developers who would embark on projects consistent with the city's plan. New London explained that this would provide a public benefit by providing an economic benefit. When some of the property owners, Susette Kelo being one, refused to sell, the NLDC seized their homes through eminent domain. The appellants in this case took issue with the use of eminent domain as specified in the Fifth Amendment.

The Court, in a 5–4 decision, decided against the appellant and allowed for eminent domain to be used in cases of economic development. The effect of the case was that private companies could seize private property so long as the seized land was developed according to government restrictions with the aim of economic improvement. The Court left it to the states whether they would allow eminent domain to be used in this fashion, what I term *post*-Kelo *eminent domain.* This decision is in stark contrast to the long line of Fourteenth Amendment cases that say the Bill of Rights applies to the states in the same fashion as it applies to the national government.

The purpose of this chapter is not to provide a critique of the Court's decision, but to see, when implementation is left to the states, what factors determine how states will react. What made some states restrict the application of post-*Kelo* eminent domain while others did not? The results support my thesis that property rights, and perhaps all rights, are no longer considered inalienable, but are considered as matters best left for legislators to decide.

III. MODEL SPECIFICATION

We know more about the impact property ownership has on political and economic conditions than we know about the political and economic conditions that impact the protection of property rights (Classens and Laeven 2003; Pipes 2003; La Porta, Lopez-de-Silanes, Shleifer, Vishny 1998, 1997). This makes model specification for this study particularly challenging because empirical researchers draw on the knowledge of those who came before.

The Court, for whatever reason, decided to let the states decide for themselves if they would allow post-*Kelo* seizures. The question that remains

Table 6.1. Categorization of States Based Upon Action Taken to Restrict *Kelo*

Passed Kelo Restricting Legislation		No Legislation Passed
Alabama	Missouri	Arkansas
Alaska	Montana	California
Arizona	Nebraska	Connecticut
Colorado	New Hampshire	Hawaii
Delaware	New Mexico	Maryland
Florida	Ohio	Massachusetts
Georgia	Pennsylvania	Mississippi
Idaho	South Dakota	Nevada
Illinois	Tennessee	New Jersey
Indiana	Texas	New York
Iowa	Vermont	North Carolina
Kansas	Virginia	North Dakota
Kentucky	West Virginia	Oklahoma
Louisiana	Wisconsin	Oregon
Maine	Wyoming	Rhode Island
Michigan		South Carolina
Minnesota		Utah
		Washington

unanswered is why some states have chosen to place an emphasis on the protection of property rights and others have not. In this analysis, a state that passed legislation to restrict post-*Kelo* eminent domain is coded one, and all others are coded zero.[1] The model specification is based upon the findings of previous studies that examine legislative voting behavior, particularly the consistent impact of interest group involvement and party affiliation at the national and state level. Table 6.1 lists the states according to whether they have passed legislation to restrict *Kelo* or not. As of 2007, thirty-two states had passed legislation, and eighteen states had not.[2]

In order to develop a proper specification that reflects the literature outlined earlier, I first look at the organized interests at the state level. To determine these interests, I examine a list of those who filed *amicus* briefs leading up to *Kelo* and also those who spoke for and against the *Kelo* decision in the congressional hearings that followed the Court's ruling. What I found is that four categories of organized interests took an active role in lobbying the Court and Congress: agriculture, construction, minority rights groups, and homeowners (Senate Hearing 109–208; House of Representatives Serial No. 109–55; *Kelo v. City of New London*).

What this study suggests by including variables for organized political interests is that organized political interests that are locked into a larger national framework—in some cases local affiliates of national organizations—have taken an active role at the state level to see their preferred position on *Kelo* adopted. As Andrew Karch explains, "[I]t is important to note that various national organizations view the dissemination of policy-relevant information as a key component of their organizational missions. . . . Interest groups also disseminate policy-relevant information . . . in addition to taking strong stands in favor of specific policies, which promotes their diffusion" (Karch 2007, p. 65). National organizations and lobbying groups are increasing their ties with their state affiliates, and the organizations in this study are no different (Thomas and Hrebenar 1992). While this is not a diffusion study, it is important to note the interstate networks that many organized interests have at their disposal as well as the link to national organizations that have a similar political goal. This study assumes that the organized interests who lobbied at the national level represent a particular constituency base that exists at the state level. For instance, a farmer in Nebraska is assumed to have the same outlook on *Kelo* as the American Farm Bureau who filed an *amicus* brief in favor of Susette Kelo and testified in Congress against the Court's ruling. This study is not arguing that organized interests lobbied state legislatures, only that knowing what side organized interests took at the national level will help us understand where citizens who are represented by those interests stand on the issue.

The threat to the American farmer goes beyond the *Kelo* decision. However, organizations representing agricultural interests saw *Kelo* as a serious threat to their way of life. These interests understood, correctly or not is not to be debated at this moment, that if the government could seize private property and turn it over to other private enterprises, then agricultural land would be threatened (American Farm Bureau Federation 2004).[3] Therefore, if a state has a large agricultural sector, as measured by the percentage of its GSP derived from agriculture (*agriculture*), that state will take action to protect property rights.[4]

Similarly, the NAACP vocally opposed the *Kelo* decision in Congress and filed an *amicus* brief leading up to the decision (NAACP 2004). The NAACP, like other groups representing minority interests, saw the decision as a threat to their group's interests. Many of the areas that would be targeted by states under the new definition of eminent domain are areas where a large number of minorities reside, thus posing a direct threat to minority homeownership and occupancy. Therefore, if the NAACP has a large presence in a state, as measured by the number of local branch offices in a state (*NAACP*), that state's government will pass legislation restricting the *Kelo* decision's application.[5]

Kelo poses a potential threat to homeowners. Kelo was a homeowner whose home was seized. Other homeowners may face the same fate as she did and therefore oppose the *Kelo* decision (New Jersey Property Owners Fighting Eminent Domain Abuse 2004; Texas Property Owners Fighting Eminent Domain Abuse 2004; Pennsylvania Property Owners Fighting Eminent Domain Abuse 2004; Hawaii Property Owners Fighting Eminent Domain Abuse 2004). The higher a state's rate of homeownership, as determined by the U.S. Census Bureau (*homeownership*), the more likely that state will be to restrict the *Kelo* decision.[6]

On the other side of the debate are construction companies. Construction companies lobbied Congress and the Court in support of the *Kelo* decision (American Planning Association 2004). "Though the use of eminent domain is critical to redevelopment projects, developers probably see no advantage to defending publicly the use of eminent domain in that context although—to be sure—they are letting their elected officials know their position" (Burke 2006, p. 669; see also Ely 2005a, p. 64). Their reason for doing so is obvious: if old structures are destroyed, and new ones are to be built, construction companies will profit. Therefore, the stronger the presence of construction interests in a state, as measured by the percentage of that state's GSP derived from construction (*construction*), the more likely that state will be to allow the *Kelo* decision to be implemented without restriction.[7]

Interested parties are not the only factors that influence legislative outcomes; party affiliation has shown to be highly influential in determining the legislation that gets through. A state with a *unified Republican govern-ment,* which is defined as a state with both governor and the majority of the legislature from the Republican Party, is expected to pass legislation restricting post-*Kelo* eminent domain for two reasons. First, unified states, regardless of party affiliation, are expected to have higher levels of coopera-tion between the executive and legislature, thus making the passage of leg-islation easier, and legislators perceive this (Bowling and Ferguson 2001). Second, Republicans were the more vocal of the two parties in opposing *Kelo.* For example, after the decision, Republican Texas Governor Rick Perry made a public statement in support of Texas's decision to prohibit post-*Kelo* seizures. Governor Perry said:

> There is no bigger supporter of economic development than I. But I draw the line when government begins to pick winners and losers among competing interests. . . . The legislation I am proud to sign today means mom-and-pop businesses and residential property must be willingly sold—not unfairly seized—when a project's purpose is private profit-making. (Perry 2005)

In addition to the public statements made by Republicans, the Republican position is also reflected in the voting coalition in *Kelo* in which the dis-senters were those justices (O'Connor, Rehnquist, Scalia, and Thomas) who are characterized as conservatives and sensitive to the Republican position. Therefore, a Republican government will be more apt to pass *Kelo*-restricting legislation because such legislative action falls in line with their party's position. Conversely, *unified Democratic government* is expected to have a negative effect on a state's decision to place restrictions on *Kelo* if we understand that the majority in *Kelo* (Stevens, Kennedy, Souter, Ginsburg, and Breyer) are typically considered to side favorably with the Democratic party's positions.[8]

In addition to constituent demand and party affiliation is a state's need for revenue. A state with a high debt, as defined by a situation in which expendi-tures exceed income (*debt*), will not restrict the *Kelo* decision.[9] As discussed earlier, the city of New London seized private property on the grounds that replacing a single-family home with private businesses or multifamily homes will increase the city's revenue, thus increasing the public good. Therefore, states with a debt will look to open new revenue streams in order to relieve their debt.

As discussed earlier, protection of property rights is not new nor distinctly American. Protection of property rights can be traced to the English common law, specifically the Magna Carta. Therefore, it is expected that states that have moved away from their common law heritage (*common law abolished*) will have less of a commitment to the common law in general, and the

protection of property rights in particular.[10] This hypothesis is derived from
the work of economists who have found that a nation's legal origin affects its
economic development and the level of protection granted to property rights
(Beck, Demirguc-Kunt, and Levine 2003; Glaeser and Shleifer 2002; La
Porta, et al. 1998; North and Thomas 1971). [11]

To date, the only attempt to quantify the common law has been by comparative economists who seek to uncover a connection between legal origin
and financial development (La Porta, et al. 1998). These researchers use
a nation's legal origin to code that nation as either common law or not.
The problem associated with coding a nation's conception of law based
upon its legal origin is that law is dynamic, thus a nation—or state—can
deviate from its foundation. A more refined measure is necessary to capture
the dynamic aspect of the law. The measure I use is based upon a state's
explicit repeal of the common law through statute or constitution. There are
states that have ended common law crimes, or refuse to recognize crimes
that are not explicitly addressed in statute or constitution—meaning the
only crimes that are considered crimes are those that are enumerated in
statute or constitution. This measure captures the dynamic nature of law by
categorizing states based upon their conception of crime in 2007 and not
at the time of their origin. This seems the most straightforward choice for
operationalizing the common law. This variable allows one to isolate those
states that have explicitly abandoned a common law foundation by writing
the common law out of their state's conception of law, and it avoids the
pitfalls associated with coding states by their legal origin.[12]

IV. RESULTS

Each of the variables reaches statistical significance and acts in the anticipated
direction. Construction and agriculture act in opposite directions, but that is to be
expected given that they each have different interests. Construction companies
benefit when there is construction, and therefore construction companies will
want to see the Court's *Kelo* decision implemented unimpeded, as it means a
greater potential for construction opportunities when the state and private companies can seize private property in order to build new businesses and residences
to serve private interests, whereas previously it was only the government who
could do so and for a more narrowly defined set of reasons. As the percentage
of a state's GSP derived from construction increases by one standard deviation
above the mean, the likelihood of that state acting to restrict *Kelo* decreases by
8.9 percent when all other values are held at their mean. Conversely, agriculture
interests perceive *Kelo* as a threat to their way of living. These interests fear that

a state will seize their land if the land can be developed into a more lucrative tax stream. Therefore, as the percentage of a state's GSP that is derived from agriculture increases, the likelihood of that state acting to restrict the *Kelo* decision increases. When all other values are held at their mean, and the value for agriculture increases by one standard deviation above its mean, the likelihood of a state acting to restrict *Kelo* increases by 3.9 percent.

Similarly, as homeownership rates increase, so too does the likelihood that a state will act to restrict the *Kelo* decision. Like agriculture interests, homeowners feel threatened by the Court's decision, as homeowners are directly affected—it was homeowners who brought the original suit to court. Homeowners fear that the Court's decision will make their homes more susceptible to seizure. While homeowners are reimbursed, most studies indicate that losing one's home to eminent domain is not a desirable or lucrative experience (Garnett 2006). Also, those interests representing minorities, in this case the NAACP, have similar fears as homeowners, as it is perceived by minority groups that areas with a high percentage of minority residents will be targeted areas for *Kelo*-type seizures. For every local NAACP branch above the mean in a state, the probability that that state will pass legislation to restrict the implementation of post-*Kelo* eminent domain increases by 15.7 percent. State governments seem to be responsive to the concerns of their citizens and act in accordance with their preferences on this topic.

Constituent demand is not all that drives government decisions. The party affiliation of government officials also influences their decisions. As expected, Republican-dominated governments are more likely to pass legislation restricting post-*Kelo* eminent domain. Compared to a divided government, a unified Republican government is more likely to pass legislation restricting *Kelo* by 11.1 percent. Conversely, the probability of a legislature passing

Table 6.2. What Factors Influence a State's Decision to Protect Property Rights?

	Coefficient	Standard Error	Probability
Construction	−0.088*	0.027	−8.9
Agriculture	0.028**	0.016	3.9
State Debt	−0.075*	0.006	−31.8
Unified Republican	0.703*	0.107	11.1
Unified Democratic	−0.063*	0.026	−9.1
Common Law Abolished	−0.111*	0.051	−1.4
Homeownership	0.017*	0.002	4.5
NAACP	0.663*	0.216	15.7

N = 50 Pseudo R^2 = 0.0621
*p < 0.01;
** p <.10% Correctly Predicted = 86%

legislation to restrict *Kelo* decreases by 9.1 percent in unified Democratic governments.

The question is raised, why—if a core supporter of the Democratic Party is opposed to *Kelo*-type seizures, such as the NAACP—is the Democratic party not the party that has acted to protect property rights? Democratic representatives were not nearly as vocal in their opposition to the *Kelo* decision as the Republican opponents to the decision were; thus, it is difficult to gauge why they oppose restrictions to post-*Kelo* seizures. One way to make sense of it is to assume that they hold the same position as those in the Court's majority. If this is the case, then what might be concluded is that state legislatures and governors have taken their cue on how to act from their ideological counterparts on the Court. Republicans voted in the manner the conservative justices on the Court voted, and Democrats at the state level voted in the manner the liberal justices on the Court voted.

Another possibility, one that addresses a core concern of this book, is that rights have become politicized, and parties have taken up the cause of some rights and not others. Democrats have not taken up the cause of property rights, much as Republicans have not taken up the cause of procedural due process rights. Rights have become politically divisive. This is a radical departure from how rights were conceived at common law and in the founding generation.

Separate from party affiliation and organized interests is fiscal demand. States in debt will look to get out of debt, and one way to do that is to increase the amount of money coming in. *Kelo* offers states the opportunity to increase their tax base by making property taxes more lucrative as the value of the developed property will be higher than the value of the property before it was seized. Therefore, it is not surprising that as the size of a state's debt increases, the likelihood of that state passing legislation to restrict *Kelo* decreases.

Lastly, and perhaps the most abstract of these variables, is common law. A state's legal heritage, I suggest, will permeate all levels of government, not just the judiciary. What the results suggest is that states that have abandoned the common law in one area are likely to abandon it in another—in this case, the protection of property rights. The legal culture of a state is an important indicator of the type of policy decisions governments make on a daily basis.

To summarize, states will pass legislation to restrict the implementation of post-*Kelo* eminent domain when the party in control of the government favors such measures, when the constituency of that state favors such measures, and when the legal culture of that state is one that respects the right to own property.

Because I categorize states as having passed restrictions as of 2007, some could criticize my findings as being out of date because states can change their status after the data were collected and analyzed for this study. To address this concern, I have included an event-history analysis (EHA) in addition to the logit model that produced the results in Table 6.2. This method of analysis has been used quite extensively by those interested in policy adoption patterns among the states. The goal of EHA is to explain what factors contribute to the occurrence of an event, and at what rate. The duration, or length of time, it takes for the event to occur is reflected in the hazard rate. The hazard rate is the likelihood of an event. A decreasing hazard—indicated in Table 6.3 by any coefficient less than 1—indicates an increasing duration, whereas an increasing hazard—any coefficient greater than 1—indicates a decreasing duration, or that the reform will come more quickly.

There is one primary advantage for using EHA over logit. EHA allows the researcher to include censored and truncated data. These are data which do not occur within the specified time frame either because they occurred before the study began or the study ends before the event occurred for a particular unit (Bennett and Stam 1996). With logit, states that adopted after 2007 would be omitted; EHA remedies this problem, and therefore no bias is introduced. For this study, it is important to handle these cases properly so as not to be criticized for being out of date. The results reported in Table 6.3 tell us why some states have acted more quickly than others to adopt legislation that prevents *Kelo*-type seizures. The categorization of the states remains the same, and the independent variables remain the same though some of the coding was altered so that the data can be analyzed through a different modeling strategy.

Table 6.3. Factors Influencing the Rapidity of Adoption

	Coefficient	Standard Error	Hazard Rate
Construction	0.670*	0.221	−33
Agriculture	1.011*	0.002	1.1
State Debt	0.302*	0.126	−69.8
Unified Republican	1.003*	0.001	0.3
Unified Democratic	0.150*	0.061	−85
Common Law Abolished	−0.111*	0.051	−88.9
Homeownership	1.121*	0.408	12.1
NAACP	1.663*	0.330	66.3

*$p < 0.01$
$N = 137$[1]

[1]For Table 3 the number of observations has increased because I use each state from 2004–2007. This means that each state has the chance to occur four times—once in each year—yielding an N of 200 if no state ever adopted legislation. But, once a state has reached failure—which means it has adopted the legislation—it is dropped from the data set because it is no longer at risk (Mintrom and Vergari 1998, p. 138 n. 14 and Box-Steffensmeier and Jones 2004). So, in this study, 32 states dropped out. This does not mean the N should be 200−32 = 168 because they did not all drop out in the same year.

Because the results in Table 6.3 only reinforce the results in Table 6.2, not much space needs to be spent interpreting the results. The final column in Table 6.3 indicates the hazard rate. This is the percentage of change associated with the coefficient in the first column. What the results show is that construction interests, state debt, a unified Democratic government, and the abolition of the common law slow down a state's effort to pass legislation that would restrict *Kelo*-type seizures. On the other hand, agriculture interests, a unified Republican government, elevated homeownership rates, and an active NAACP increase the hazard rate, meaning those factors increase the speed with which a state will adopt legislation that will restrict *Kelo*-type seizures. This is precisely what is seen in Table 6.2, which means the same conclusions can be drawn.

V. DISCUSSION

The results are not surprising in that state governments pass legislation that accurately reflects the demands of their party affiliation and the more vocal members of their constituency. Those who perceive *Kelo* as a threat to their property rights made their position known, just as those who anticipate a profit from *Kelo* made theirs known. But, more than just constituent demands and party affiliation condition voting behavior: the legal culture and fiscal needs of a state influence the type of legislation passed.

The one surprising result might be that the Democratic Party at the state level has run away from the NAACP. One of the interesting hypotheses that come out of this study that has not been fully explored is the degree to which state legislatures and governors take cues from the national government, particularly the Supreme Court. While there is research to suggest judges on State Courts of Last Resort take into consideration the Supreme Court's position, or anticipated position, on a particular issue, less is known about the influence Supreme Court voting patterns have on other political actors at the state level.

When considering that Democrats on the Court and in the states support *Kelo*, and Republicans at both levels oppose the decision, one should recall that such a division over property rights did not exist during the early years of the republic. This chapter shows just how far the nation has come in its understanding of property rights, not just in the obvious sense, but also in how they are conceptualized by government officials. Rights are no longer inalienable or universal truths, but instead are planks in a party platform. While Democrats have tended to concern themselves with civil liberties, Republicans have concerned themselves with economic liberties.[13] Both sides have a narrow view of rights and liberties—or worse. Perhaps the only thing worse than this scenario is if the parties care not about rights at all, but only about being able to form a winning coalition, and have therefore attached themselves to a set of rights to win votes and not because of a genuine concern for the protection of the rights. In any event, the politicization of rights has threatened their preservation. It is one thing to think one set of rights is more important than another, but quite another thing to say that one right ought to be sacrificed in favor of another. As shown in chapters 3 and 4, the founding generation—and Locke—argued that the inalienable rights that our government is designed to protect do not exist independent from one another and one right cannot survive without the preservation of the others.

The Court left it for the states to decide, and those states that want to protect property rights have done so, and those that do not, have not. The Court is not the final arbiter of property rights in this context, and those who blame the Court for its assault on property rights should turn their attention to state governments that have not passed legislation limiting the implementation of *Kelo*. But, the concern is still present that if rights are not seen as inalienable, but rather are seen as political issues, the threat to rights is still present.

NOTES

1. Logit will be used as this is the dependent variable. Restrict Kelo: If a legislature passed legislation that was approved by the governor by 2007 that was aimed directly at restricting the *Kelo* decision, that state is coded 1 (National Conference of State Legislatures).

2. I define "passed legislation" as that legislation that has gone through the legislature, the governor, and has been enacted into law. The list of states that have taken action would grow if I were to apply a looser restriction and count those states that have legislation proposed but not yet enacted. Because this is a new issue and legislation is pending, these numbers will change after 2007. But, the reason for passing legislation will not. Moreover, I adopt an EHA to protect against dated results.

3. This study does not examine the validity of the claims of the organized interests cited in this study. All this study is saying is that the constituency of voters those interests represent, if strong enough, can influence government decisions.

4. Agriculture: This is the percentage of a state's GSP derived from agriculture (Statistical Abstract of the United States).

5. NAACP: This is the number of NAACP branches in a state (NAACP website).

6. Homeownership: This variable indicates the homeownership rates by state (U.S. Census Bureau).

7. Construction: This is the percentage of a state's GSP derived from construction (Statistical Abstract of the United States).

8. Unified Republican and Unified Democratic: This is a dummy variable indicating when a state's legislature and governor are controlled by the Republican party or Democratic party (*Book of the States*). I did not use a measure for liberalism as the question of property rights is not a liberal or conservative issue but is a matter of party affiliation. It is not possible to place a liberal or conservative tag on an issue that puts Libertarians and farmers on the same side of the debate.

9. State Debt: This is the total dollar value of the difference between state income and expenditures. Debt is when the expenditures are greater than the income (Statistical Abstract of the United States).

10. Common Law Abolished: The explicit rejection of common law crimes by a state either in statute or constitution: (1) if abolished, (0) otherwise (Various state constitutions and statutes).

11. These researchers have found that the common law arose in England as a response to the Crown's oppression; whereas the civil law system that arose in France was the result of local lords fearing one another more than the Crown (Glaeser and Shleifer 2002, p. 1193). This means, when it came to adjudicating cases, more power was to be placed into the hands of the state in the civil law system when compared to the common law system: as a result, codification also became a hallmark of the civil law system (Glaeser and Shleifer 2002, p. 1211).

12. One variable not included that one might wish to see is public opinion. First, data is not available for all fifty states. The surveys taken have been at the national level or exist for only a few states. Second, liberalism scores are unreliable in this context. Property rights, as I have argued, bridge traditional ideological gaps. Those typically referred to as liberals, for instance, NAACP, and those typically categorized as conservative, homeowners, are on the same side of the debate. The property right debate finds Libertarians and farmers on the same side of the debate, though they typically are at polar extremes. Therefore, typical measures of policy liberalism do not capture the transcendent nature of property rights. This is why, to review, the party in power is used and not a liberalism score for the government.

13. I acknowledge that both parties have undergone realignments that have changed their positions, but the current party system, since 1957, is the party dynamic I am referencing—with the exception of Southern Democrats.

Chapter 7

Implications

Up to this point, I have made the argument that property rights are valuable because those people and ideas that shaped our Constitution have found them valuable. Along the way, I have pointed to philosophical, historical, and legal justifications for the protection of property. The justification for the protection of property rights appeals to the philosophical, historical, legal, and material. The first three justifications have been discussed in the previous six chapters; a discussion of the material has been left for last. This chapter engages those who want a more concrete answer to the "so what" question.

There is a clear connection between economic prosperity and property rights. Therefore, states that have acted to restrict the use of *Kelo*-type takings should enjoy greater economic prosperity. This chapter summarizes the literature on this topic and provides its own contribution to the debate. Unfortunately, because *Kelo* is so recent, not enough time has elapsed to provide a comprehensive analysis of the effect a state's reaction to *Kelo* has had on its economic prosperity, due to the fact that there is an anticipated time lag between the inception of a law and its impact on the economy. That said, the chapter provides results and direction for future research.

This chapter develops in three sections. Section I discusses the necessity of property rights for economic prosperity. Section II discusses the institutional arrangements necessary to protect property rights. Section III discusses the effect state reactions to the *Kelo* decision have had on the economic growth of the state. Drawing on Sections I and II, Section III explores the question of whether states that have not restricted the application of *Kelo* have violated the institutional arrangements necessary for the protection of property rights, thereby sacrificing economic prosperity.

I. PROPERTY RIGHTS AND ECONOMIC PROSPERITY

Property rights are a powerful incentive for the creation of wealth. Secure property rights give investors confidence that if gains are made, the investor will receive those gains. Moreover, if one owns property, one is more likely to invest in and improve one's property. If the property rights are precarious, and the investor is unlikely to reap the rewards of their investment, investment is unlikely. Property ownership in nineteenth-century America represents the link between economy and property as it incorporated possession, use, and transfer (Ely 2005, p. 490).[1] Economists have concluded that "[c]apitalism relies heavily on markets and private property rights to resolve conflicts over the use of scarce resources" (Alchian and Demsetz 1973, p. 16). However, if property rights are threatened, they cannot perform this function. This section surveys the current economic literature to show that there is a clear connection between economic growth and the protection of property rights.

Stijin Claesens and Luck Laeven (2003) show that in countries with more secure property rights, firms allocate resources better and consequently grow faster as the returns on different types of assets are assured. Secure property rights likely lead to reinvestment of profits (Claesens and Laeven 2003, p. 2401). "A firm is always at risk of not getting the returns from its assets due to actions by the government, its own employees, or other firms. . . . As such, property rights in a narrow sense are very important for securing returns. . . . More generally, we argue that the degrees to which firms allocate resources in an optimal way will depend on the strength of a country's property rights" (Claesens and Laeven 2003, p. 2402–2403). Firms do not like threats to their assets, nor do they like uncertainty on the return of their assets. Therefore, in countries with secure property rights, threats and uncertainty are minimized, and firms are likely to act by reinvesting their assets. The predicted result of a government making property rights less secure for firms and property owners will be a decrease in investment.

Timothy Besley (1995) draws a similar conclusion by showing that ownership rights provide investment incentives. So, while Claesens and Laeven focused almost exclusively on intangible assets, Besley finds a similar result with private ownership of tangible property. Besley's conclusion rests on the Lockean theory of property rights that what one mixes its labor with becomes his or hers. The more secure property rights, the greater the incentive to invest, because individuals do not invest if the fruits of their labor are seized by others. Better rights make it easier to use land for collateral, and investment is encouraged if improved transfer rights make it easier for individuals to rent or sell their land (Besley 1995, p. 906–907). The empirical results from his study support the theory when he finds that "tree planting in Wassa found investments significantly related to land rights. . . . In all cases, except continuous manuring and irrigation, the rights variables have a positive and significant effect on the probability of investing" (Besley 1995, p. 926–927). While investing in farms and trees may not sound significant, economic growth cannot sustain, or even get off the ground, without these types of investments. Moreover, this study lends credence to the fears of *Kelo* critics who worry about both the deleterious effects post-*Kelo* eminent domain will have on individual property ownership and the subsequent repercussions. That is, there is a concern that homeowners and small business owners will be hesitant to make efforts to invest in their property if there is a greater potential for their property to be seized.

In a follow-up study, Besley and Robin Burgess (2000) find that land reforms directed at making individual land acquisition easier increases economic growth and decreases poverty. "By affecting access to land, land reform may have a more lasting effect on poverty. This view is consistent with the literature that points to early redistributions of land leading to relatively egalitarian access as being an important precondition for high growth in East Asia" (Besley and Burgess 2000, p. 391). India has gone the opposite direction of the United States by extending property ownership to a class of citizens to whom *Kelo* effectively restricts the path to property ownership.

Simon Johnson, John McMillan, and Christopher Woodruff (2002) build on the economic literature that has found "Property rights are fundamental: entrepreneurs will not invest if they expect to be unable to keep the fruits of their investment. Country-level studies consistently show that less secure property rights are correlated with lower aggregate investment and slower economic growth" (Johnson, McMillan, and Woodruff 2002, p. 1335). The authors find that, "Firms' investment is affected by the perceived security of property rights, as shown by both our cross-country data and firm-level regressions" (Johnson, McMillan, and Woodruff 2002, p. 1354). These findings confirm the findings of the other studies discussed and help integrate the work of those who focus only on firms and those who focus only on individual investors by demonstrating that both firms and individual investors are susceptible to the same influences when it comes to property rights. Johnson et al. rely on survey responses from firms which allow the researchers to tap into the concerns of the individual as an individual as well as an actor within a firm. The Johnson et al. study demonstrates that it is both large firms and individuals who might feel threatened by the *Kelo* decision, and thus restrict investment, as *Kelo* only says that property can be seized by the government and turned over to a private owner if it will increase the public good. Neither firms nor individuals are given preference in the *Kelo* decision.

Gerald O'Driscoll and Lee Hoskins (2003) claim that "The difference between prosperity and poverty is property" (O'Driscoll and Hoskins 2003, p. 2). While their study seems to lack the theoretical development that the other articles do, the authors provide some interesting accounts of when this connection has been seen. Their most persuasive point is made when they show that "On average, GDP per capita, measured in terms of purchasing power parity, is twice as high in nations with the strongest protection of property than in those providing only fairly good protections. Once the protection of property shows clear signs of deterioration . . . GDP per capita drops to a fifth of that in countries with the strongest protection" (O'Driscoll and Hoskins 2003, p. 9).

O'Driscoll and Hoskins rest their understanding of the link between prosperity and property on F. A. Hayek's account. "The system of private property is the most important guarantee of freedom. . . . It is only because the control of the means of production is divided among many people acting independently that nobody has complete power over us, that we as individuals can decide what to do with ourselves" (Hayek 1944, p. 103). Unfortunately, Hayek, and by extension O'Driscoll and Hoskins, fail to elaborate on the causal mechanism. Hayek's account is consistent with Locke who also says that secure property will increase cultivation. From those who have provided a rich theoretical account of the link between property and prosperity, it is clear that secure property rights instill a sense of security in people that they will see returns on their investments. While investment is not without risk even in nations with secure property rights, the risk is minimized because the arbitrary taking of property through force or coercion is minimized. Therefore, people feel secure when their property is secure, people will seek to cultivate and invest in their property when they feel secure, and the resulting cultivation and investment leads to economic growth. What follows is a discussion of those institutions and legal structures that researchers have found to be successful at securing property rights.

II. INSTITUTIONS AND PROPERTY

Economic historians have consistently noted the link between institutions, property, and economic development. It has been observed that a relative rise in the value of land in twelfth-century England led to efforts to convert the existing right structure into one that allowed for exclusive ownership and transferability (North and Thomas 1971, p. 25). Douglass North has found that the most influential factor in determining the structure of property rights is the state. Institutions that have been the most successful at protecting property rights developed out of the need to protect people and their property from government infringement. The rules and institutions protecting property could not be arbitrary or capricious; people demanded that their property be protected through settled and known laws and institutions. "The strengthening of the institutions of private property consisted to a very important degree in legally limiting the power of government. The objective was to embody a set of comprehensive rules in an impersonal legal structure—rules that would not be subject to political whim and change by legislative bodies" (North 1981, p. 189–190). When such institutions are in place, property rights are secure and economic growth results. "Ultimately it is the state that is responsible for the efficiency of the property rights structure, which causes growth or stagnation or economic decline" (North 1981, p. 17).

Like many academics, it is sometimes difficult to pin North down to a specific economic and government system that will maximize economic growth. That is, it would be difficult to use North's writings as an outline for a constitution. But, we know from his research that government involvement beyond protection can lead to economic stagnation. Countries that allow the most valuable rights—such as property rights—to remain in the public domain tend to have a citizenry that does not act to capture or capitalize on those rights (North 1990, p. 33). "Secure property rights will require political and judicial organizations that effectively and impartially enforce contracts across space and time" (North 1990, p. 121). This is precisely the concern of *Kelo* critics. The accusation is that the Court did not decide the case impartially, nor did the justices apply a strict reading of the Constitution to the matter. While the impartiality of the Court has not been tested in this book, what has been shown is that state legislatures have not acted impartially when deciding whether to allow *Kelo* acquisitions or prohibit *Kelo*-type seizures. Besides legal culture, economic interests and party affiliation are the most prominent factors in determining whether a state would act to protect property rights. Such factors hardly give the impression that decisions regarding *Kelo* are impartial.

Edward Glaeser and Andrei Shleifer (2002) build on North's historical analysis by developing a formal model that suggests "For a legal system to protect property, the effects of coercion and corruption must be limited" (Glaeser and Shleifer 2002, p. 1195). As outlined in chapter 6, Glaeser and Shleifer find that legal systems founded in the common law tradition are more effective at protecting property rights. The authors suggest that a central goal of the legal system is to protect legitimacy and prevent corruption and rule by force. This goes two ways: legal enforcers need to be protected from bands of bullies, and citizens need to be protected from arbitrarily harsh rule by the government. In France, the feudal lords were powerful and thus were able to exert influence on local justice officials. In England, the lords were less powerful and thus more concerned with oppression from the Crown. Therefore, when bullying is moderate—in the case of England—it is more efficient to let the local magistrates and juries handle matters. But, when the bullying is extreme, adjudication must be placed in the hands of state officials, which potentially leads to greater politicization of the legal process. France's concern with feudal conflict led to the development of the civil law system, and England's concern with oppression from the Crown led to the development of the common law system (Glaeser and Shleifer 2002, p. 1195).

Characteristics of the common law system, such as the adversarial system, separation between judge and prosecution, and a jury system, demonstrate that the concern was with the government, not the people. At common law, power is placed in the hands of local magistrates that determine right and wrong based on past legal decisions. A jury is only legitimate when the public perceives the jury as free from outside tampering. Juries, being of the people, consistently acted to protect property rights, as they understood the link between property and liberty. In France, under the civil code, laws were codified, and thus authority was taken out of the hands of the people— because that is where the threat was perceived to come from—and placed in the hands of the government. As a result, property rights became less secure as the government sought to limit the power of the lords by limiting their property rights. Legal origin determines current economic progress if the legal origin remains largely in place.

> At the same level of development, French civil law countries exhibit heavier regulation, less secure property rights, more corrupt and less efficient governments, and even less political freedom than do common law countries. . . . One area where the greater insecurity of property rights in civil law countries shows up clearly is the development of financial markets. On just about every measure, common law countries are more financially developed than civil law countries. (Glaeser and Shleifer 2002, p. 1194)

There is no need to go further into the relationship between the common law and property as that discussion took place in chapter 1. But, it is interesting to note that economic historians, and quantitative economists, have each found that property rights are more secure when government infringement is minimized.

Other researchers have found that a country's legal origin plays a role in how well it protects certain financial rights, particularly property rights. Legal origins are also important for financial development because institutions vary in their ability to adapt efficiently to evolving economic conditions (Beck, Demirguc-Kunt, and Levine 2003, p. 653). The political channel of the law and finance literature contends that legal traditions differ in terms of the priority they attach to private property rights versus the rights of the state, and that the protection of private contracting rights forms the basis of financial development (Beck, Demirguc-Kunt, and Levine 2003, p. 654). Similar to the account provided by Glaeser and Shleifer, Beck et al. suggest that, according to the political channel thesis, English common law evolved to protect private property owners against the Crown. In contrast, the political channel holds that the French and German civil codes in the nineteenth century were constructed to solidify state power by placing the prince above the law (Beck, Demirguc-Kunt, and Levine 2003, p. 654). While not explicitly stated by Glaeser and Shleifer, Beck et al. conclude that the differentiating characteristic of the civil and common law systems is the amount of control over the judiciary granted to the state (Beck, Demirguc-Kunt, and Levine 2003, p. 655). Therefore, "over time, state dominance of the judiciary produced legal traditions that focus more on the power of the state and less on the rights of the individual investors" (Beck, Demirguc-Kunt, and Levine 2003, p. 654–655). Therefore, those legal structures that place power to settle disputes in the hands of the people will provide greater protection for property rights. By securing property rights, these legal structures help secure economic growth. The underlying theme is that when people feel in control and free from coercion or arbitrary rule, law and economics work in concert to provide prosperity.

III. *KELO'S* EFFECT ON STATE ECONOMIC GROWTH

Kelo follows a similar pattern as that studied by Besley and Burgess (2000) in India. Like *Kelo* in the United States, the India constitution allowed states to determine for themselves when and how they would enact land reform. And because there were no time restrictions, the variation in the adoption pattern allowed for a comparative analysis of property reform within India. "The fact that land reforms were a state subject under the 1949 Constitution meant that enactment and implementation was dependent on the political will of state governments" (Besley and Burgess 2000, p. 394). The *Kelo* decision allows for the same sort of comparative analysis as carried out in chapter 6, but because economic patterns that are dependent upon legal reform do not happen instantaneously, charting an effect becomes difficult in the short time span of two years. Therefore, at this point multivariate time-series analysis cannot be employed. But, simple comparisons between states that have passed legislation to restrict *Kelo* seizures and those that have not can provide some insight into the effect a state's decision to restrict *Kelo* has had on the state economy.

Table 7.1.   Top 10 GSP Growth from 2004–2007

Restriction States	*Non-Restriction States*
Idaho (1)	Utah (2)
Arizona (3)	Oklahoma (4)
Colorado (8)	North Dakota (6)
Montana (9)	Oregon (7)
New Mexico (5)	
Texas (10)	

Source: (Data Source: Bureau of Economic Analysis; State Rank in Parentheses)

The Bureau of Economic Analysis (BEA) compiles yearly statistics for state economic growth, which is measured as the increase in Gross State Product (GSP) in the current year over the previous year. The BEA provides the data necessary to derive this for per capita (GSPP) as well. But rather than compare the current year with the previous year, I chart growth from 2004—the year preceding *Kelo*—to 2007—two years post-*Kelo*. Six of the top ten growth states from 2004 to 2007, measured as change in GSP, were states that passed restrictions on *Kelo* seizures. When growth is measured as GSPP, only five of the top ten growth states had passed *Kelo* restrictions. In terms of economic growth, as measured by GSP and GSPP, there seems to be little evidence that legislation restricting *Kelo* has made any impact on economic growth at the state level.

A third indicator employed to help discern what impact *Kelo* legislation has had at the state level is homeownership. Based on previous research, one would anticipate that homeownership rates would decrease if the state allowed for *Kelo* seizures. And that is precisely what occurs. Homeownership rates by state are derived from the U.S. Census Bureau, just as they were in chapter 6. When comparing the current homeownership rates of 2007 between the two categories of states, the difference is not large. But when the change in ownership rates is calculated for the two categories of states, a more complete story unfolds. Homeownership rates in states that passed restrictions on *Kelo* seizures increased, and other states saw a decrease in homeownership rates. Homeownership increased nearly 3.0 percent more in restriction states than

Table 7.2.   Top 10 GSPP Growth from 2004–2007

Restriction States	*Non-Restriction States*
Delaware (1)	Connecticut (2)
Colorado (6)	Massachusetts (3)
Alaska (7)	New York (4)
Virginia (8)	New Jersey (5)
Minnesota (10)	California (9)

Source: (Data Source: Bureau of Economic Analysis; State Rank in Parentheses)

Table 7.3. Homeownership Rates

Rates for 2007	
Restriction States	*Non-Restriction States*
68.1%	67.8%
Rate of Change from 2004–2007	
Restriction States	*Non-Restriction States*
+1.6%	−1.2%

Source: (Data Source: U.S. Census Bureau)

non-restriction states, thus indicating that people in states that do not allow *Kelo*-type seizures feel more secure in their right to own property, and thus more secure that their home will be protected from government seizure.

There is more to economic growth than merely increasing GSP and increasing the rate of homeownership. Economists have found that the protection of property rights also has an impact on the poverty rate. Therefore, when comparing poverty rates between the two categories of states, those states that provide greater protection of property rights have nearly identical poverty rates as their counterparts in 2007, but the change in poverty rate tells a different story. States that have taken positive action to protect property rights have seen a decrease in their poverty rate greater than in states that have not taken action. And while the reduction in the poverty rate has not been overwhelming in restriction states, these states have outperformed non-restriction states by nearly 2 percent. This might indicate that the growth seen in restriction states has not been driven by elite growth but by an increase among the most disadvantaged among the state's population.

The conclusions that can be drawn from these comparisons are limited and must be conditioned by an acknowledgment of the short period since the *Kelo* decision. Critics of the *Kelo* decision should not feel discouraged because of the modest results, and proponents of the decision should not feel victorious. The comparisons do show a trend in the anticipated direction of increased economic well-being as a result of property rights protection.

Table 7.4. Poverty Rates

Rates for 2007	
Restriction States	*Non-Restriction States*
11.9%	11.9%
Rate of Change from 2004–2007	
Restriction States	*Non-Restriction States*
−0.4%	+1.5%

Source: (Data Source: U.S. Census Bureau)

Homeownership rates are on the increase and poverty is on the decrease in states that have taken positive action to protect property rights. And while traditional indicators of economic growth do not show a significant difference between the two categories of states, it should once again be stated that the reason for this might be due to the fact that the decision was so recent. Researchers expect the most significant economic growth as a result of legislation to occur between five and ten years after the legislation has taken effect (Christainsen and Haveman 1981; Denison 1979). Therefore, it would be irresponsible to reach a definitive conclusion based upon the current research.[2]

That said, opponents of *Kelo* can find some preliminary support for the position that the correlation between the protection of property rights and economic growth is a positive one, and states that choose not to restrict the application of *Kelo* risk sacrificing economic growth. Moreover, there is more empirical, historical, and theoretical support for the connection between property rights and economic prosperity than exists on the opposing side. Those who favor *Kelo*—which includes the Court and as argued by the City of New London—did so on the grounds that there would be a direct economic gain. In light of these results, their constitutional argument was misguided, and their practical argument was unfounded.

This chapter has set out to do nothing more than provide a reason for those who are unconvinced by theoretical and legal arguments of the importance of property rights. And while the arguments made in chapters 1 through 5 form a powerful criticism of the *Kelo* decision by explicating the connection between property and liberty that the decision violates, this chapter has added an additional layer to the argument. In the course of making the argument that the protection of property rights can bring about economic gains, this chapter has shown that there are opportunities for interdisciplinary research that explore the relationship between law, economics, and politics.

NOTES

1. In his dissenting opinion in *Munn v. Illinois,* Stephen J. Field wrote, "All that is beneficial in property arises from its use, and the fruits of that use; and whatever deprives a person of them deprives him of all that is desirable or valuable in the title and possession" (94 U.S. 113, 141 (1877)).

2. A recent study for the Institute of Justice by Carpenter and Ross demonstrates that there has been no economic advantage—as measured by economic health, property tax revenue, and construction projects—bestowed on states that perform *Kelo*-type seizures, thus leading them to conclude that the economic benefit anticipated by

Kelo proponents was inaccurate (Carpenter and Ross 2008). This study is valuable in directing our attention to an important area of study, but it does not engage the expansive literature on the link between institutions, property, and prosperity even though it empirically addresses the question. Moreover, the authors do not take into account the necessary time lag between legislative action and economic response. The authors of this study apply a hierachical-linear model (HLM)—a more sophisticated strategy than the one I have employed to be sure—but reach the same conclusion in that there is no definitive answer with regard to legislation and economic prosperity. Had the authors included an analysis of what happens to homeownership and poverty rates, and not just economic health, construction, and property tax revenue, then they might have noticed that the legislation does have some effect on the economy, even within the short time table under consideration. With all that being said, the authors of this study and myself are on the same side of the debate with regard to what effect illegitimate property seizures are likely to have on the economy. My only reservation with their study is that they do not fully engage the theoretical debate or take into account the time lag. But, their effort goes a long way in refuting the claims of developers and city officials who advocate *Kelo*-type seizures on the grounds that it will lead to greater economic prosperity. Surely, if the authors continue their research in this area, they will continue to make similar substantive gains.

Conclusion

The 2005 Supreme Court decision *Kelo v. City of New London* gener-
ated more public outrage than most Supreme Court decisions. The reason
for the outrage was the curtailment of constitutionally protected property
rights. While a debate on this issue is good, the historical and normative
foundations of property rights are often ignored, thus leaving many
opinions on this issue ill-informed. This book has tried to remedy many
of the deficiencies that exist in popular and academic publications. For
instance, this book has successfully refuted the common view that "very
little historical material exists from which to ascertain the framers' intent
[with regard to the Fifth Amendment] . . . neither colonial practice nor
Foundering Era philosophy was clear" (Gold 1999, p. 181). In light of the
research I have presented, such comments can be categorized as fallacious.
This project also has provided empirical and normative support for its legal
and historical arguments.

This book discussed what happens when rights that were once considered
inalienable become debatable and mutable. At the time of the founding,
there was a near consensus on the importance of property rights, and for the
architect of the Bill of Rights and the delegates at state constitutional conventions before and after 1787, there was an agreement that all rights were
inextricably linked. Modern politics has failed to see the unity of rights, as
advocates for one set of rights are often of a different ideological predisposi-
tion than advocates for another set of rights, which then makes each side see
the other side—and the interests they represent—as a threat. The result is that
the promotion of rights becomes a zero-sum game in which some rights are
promoted at the expense of others. By exploring this issue in the context of
Kelo v. City of New London, I have shown how this development has placed

145

property rights in jeopardy. I have shown that the politicization of rights has weakened the protection they offer against government action.

Politics can be a good thing. But when it comes to rights, politics are damaging. When rights are treated like every other political issue, they cease to serve their purpose. Rights are protections against the government and people. When the government takes charge of rights, the people cannot protect themselves against the government. Rights should be respected by, not defined by, the political process. If rights are not absolute and independent, they cannot fulfill their intended purpose and instead become rhetorical flourishes.

This project has taken the issue as far as it can, but that does not mean there is not more work to be done. Research should build on this study to look at the effect a two-party system has on rights and whether such a political system, while stable and perhaps inevitable in an American-style government, is desirable with regard to rights. This work can be extended into discussions of civil society and deliberative democracy. We should examine whether rights, like organized groups and other competing interests, necessarily move to entrench themselves within the political system—and force out the competition—in order to maximize their advantage. If this is the case, then we might be forced to question the ability of democracy to protect rights in particular instances rather than in the aggregate. We must critically examine the assumptions of *Federalist #10* to understand whether making everything political is advantageous for rights. Ironically, it may be found that the process by which Madison sought to protect property rights might lead to their destruction.

I think it is best to conclude with the words of Justice Potter Stewart in *Lynch v. Household Finance Corporation* (1972):

> Such difficulties indicate that the dichotomy between personal liberties and property rights is a false one. Property does not have rights. People have rights. The right to enjoy property without unlawful deprivation, no less than the right to speak or the right to travel, is in truth a "personal" right, whether the "property" in question be a welfare check, a home, or a savings account. In fact, a fundamental interdependence exists between the personal right to liberty and the personal right in property. Neither could have meaning without the other. That rights in property are basic civil rights has long been recognized.

Bibliography

Adams, John, *The Works of John Adams*. Vol. 6. ed. Charles Francis Adams. Boston, MA: Little, Brown, 1851.

Adams, Willi Paul, *The First American Constitutions: Republican Ideology and the Making of the State Constitutions in the Revolutionary Era*. Trans. Rita and Robert Kimber. Chapel Hill, NC: University of North Carolina Press, 1980.

Alchian, Armen A., and Harold Demsetz. "The Property Rights Paradigm." *The Journal of Economic History* 33, no. 1 (1973).

Alschuler, Albert W. *Law without Values*. Chicago, IL: The University of Chicago Press, 2000.

Alschuler, Albert W. "Rediscovering Blackstone." *University of Pennsylvania Law Review* 145, no. 1 (November 1996): 1–54.

Amar, Akhil Reed. *The Bill of Rights: Creation and Reconstruction*. New Haven, CT: Yale University Press, 1998.

American Farm Bureau Federation. *Amici Curiae to the United States Supreme Court in* Susette Kelo v. City of New London, 2004.

American Planning Association. *Amici Curiae to the United States Supreme Court in* Susette Kelo v. City of New London, 2004.

Ashcraft, Richard. *Revolutionary Politics and Locke's* Two Treatises of Government. Princeton, NJ: Princeton University Press, 1986.

Bailyn, Bernard. *Ideological Origins of the American Revolution*. Cambridge, MA: Harvard University Press, 1967.

Banning, Lance. *The Jeffersonian Persuasion: Evolution of a Party Ideology*. Ithaca, NY: Cornell University Press, 1978.

Beard, Charles A. *An Economic Interpretation of the Constitution of the United States*. New York, NY: Macmillan, 1913.

Beck, Thorsten, Asli Demirguc-Kunt, and Ross Levine. "Law and Finance: Why Does Legal Origin Matter?" *Journal of Comparative Economics* 31, no. 3 (2003): 653–675.

Becker, Carl. *The Declaration of Independence: A Study in the History of Political Ideas.* New York, NY: Vintage Books, 1942.

Bennett, D. Scott, and Allan C. Stam III. "The Duration of Interstate Wars, 1816–1985." *The American Political Science Review,* 90, no. 2 (June 1996): 239–257.

Besley, Timothy, and Robin Burgess. "Land Reform, Poverty Reduction, and Growth: Evidence from India." *The Quarterly Journal of Economics,* 115, no. 2 (May 2000): 389–430.

Besley, Timothy. "Property Rights and Investment Incentives: Theory and Evidence from Ghana." *The Journal of Political Economy,* 103, no. 5 (October 1995): 903–937.

Blackstone, William. *Commentaries on the Laws of England.* 4 volumes. ed. William G. Hammond. San Francisco, CA: Bancroft-Whitney, 1890.

Boorstin, Daniel J. *The Mysterious Science of the Law: An Essay on Blackstone's Commentaries.* Chicago, IL: University of Chicago Press, 1996.

Bowling, Cynthia J., and Margaret R. Ferguson. "Divided Government, Interest Representation, and Policy Differences: Competing Explanations of Gridlock in the Fifty States." *Journal of Politics,* 63, no. 1 (February 2001): 182–206.

Box-Steffensmeier, Janet M., and Bradford S. Jones. *Event History Modeling: A Guide for Social Scientists.* New York, NY: Cambridge University Press, 2004.

Burke, Marcilynn A. "Much Ado about Nothing: *Kelo v. City of New London, Babbitt v. Sweet Home,* and Other Tales from the Supreme Court." *University of Cincinnati Law Review.* 75(2006): 663–723.

Burstein, Paul, and April Linton. "The Impact of Political Parties, Interest Groups, and Social Movement Organizations on Public Policy: Some Recent Evidence and Theoretical Concerns." *Social Forces,* 81, no. 2 (2002): 380–408.

Carey, George W., and James McClellan. *The Federalist.* Indianapolis, IN: Liberty Fund, Inc, 2001.

Carpenter, Dick M., and John K. Ross. *Doomsday? No Way: Economic Trends and Post-Kelo Eminent Domain Reform.* Arlington, VA: Institute for Justice, 2008.

Carrese, Paul O. *The Cloaking of Power.* Chicago, IL: The University of Chicago Press, 2003.

Cherno, Melvin. "Locke on Property: A Reappraisal." *Ethics,* 68, no. 1 (October 1957): 51–55.

Christainsen, Gregory B., and Robert H. Haveman. "Public Regulations and the Slowdown in Productivity Growth." *American Economic Review,* 71, no. 2 (May 1981): 320–325.

Claessens, Stijn, and Luc Laeven. "Financial Development, Property Rights, and Growth." *Journal of Finance,* 58, no. 6 (December 2003): 2401–2463.

Clark, John A., and Kevin T. McGuire. 1996. "Congress, the Supreme Court, and the Flag." *Political Research Quarterly,* 49, no. 1 (1996): 771–781.

Coke, Edward. *The Selected Writings of Sir Edward Coke.* 3 volumes. ed. Steve Sheppard. Indianapolis, IN: Liberty Fund, Inc, 2004.

Coke, Edward. *The First Part of the Institutes of the Laws of England.* 18th ed. Lawbook Exchange, 1999.

Coke, Edward. *An Abridgement of the Lord Coke's Commentary on Littleton.* ed., Sir Humphrey Davenport. New York, NY: Garland Publishing, 1979.

Coke, Edward. *The Second Part of the Institutes of the Laws of England: Containing the Exposition of Many Ancient and Other Statutes.* Omni Publications, 1974.

Cooley, Thomas. *A Treatise on the Constitutional Limitations Which Rest upon the Legislative Power of the States of the American Union.* Boston, MA: Little, Brown, 1868.

Corwin, Edward S. "'The Higher Law' Background of American Constitutional Law." *Harvard Law Review,* 42, no. 1 (1928).

Denison, Edward F. "Pollution Abatement Programs: Estimates of Their Effect upon Output per Unit of Input, 1975–1978." *Survey of Current Business.* (1979).

Dumbauld, Edward. *The Bill of Rights and What It Means Today.* Norman, OK: University of Oklahoma, 1957.

Ely, James W. "'Poor Relation' Once More: The Supreme Court and the Vanishing Rights of Property Owners." *Cato Supreme Court Review, 2004–2005.* Washington, D.C.: Cato Institute, 2005a.

Ely, James W. "Property Rights and Democracy in the American Constitutional Order." in *The Judicial Branch.* ed., Kermit L Hall and Kevin T. McGuire. New York, NY: Oxford University Press, 2005b.

Ely, James W. *The Guardian of Every Other Right: A Constitutional History of Property Rights.* New York, NY: Oxford University Press, 1998.

Epstein, Richard A. *Takings: Private Property and the Power of Eminent Domain.* Cambridge, MA: Harvard University Press, 1985.

Garnett, Nicole Steel. "The Neglected Political Economy of Eminent Domain." *University of Michigan Law Review,* 105 (October 2006): 101–150.

Gedicks, Frederick Mark. "An Originalist Defense of Substantive Due Process: Magna Carta, Higher-Law Constitutionalism, and the Fifth Amendment." *Emory Law Journal,* 58, no. 2 (2009): 585–673.

Glaeser, Edward L., and Andrei Shleifer. "Legal Origins." *The Quarterly Journal of Economics,* 117, no. 4 (November 2002): 1193–1229.

Gold, Andrew S. "Regulatory Takings and Original Intent: The Direct, Physical Takings Thesis 'Goes Too Far.'" *American University Law Review,* 49 (1999): 181.

Gold, David M. "Eminent Domain and Economic Development: The Mill Acts and the Origins of Laissez-Fair Constitutionalism." *Journal of Libertarian Studies,* 21, no. 2 (Summer 2007): 101–122.

Goldberg, John C. P. "The Constitutional Status of Tort Law: Due Process and the Right to a Law for the Redress of Wrongs." *Vanderbilt Public Law Research Paper No. 05–27,* 2005.

Gough, J. W. *Fundamental Law in English Constitutional History.* Oxford, UK: Clarendon Press, 1971.

Grofman, Bernard, Robert Griffin, and Amihai Glazer. "Is the Senate More Liberal than the House? Another Look." *Legislative Studies Quarterly,* 16, no. 2 (May 1991): 281–295.

Hamilton, Alexander. *The Records of the Federal Convention of 1787.* Vol. 1. ed., Max Farrand. New Haven, CT: Yale University Press, 1937.

Hartz, Louis. *The Liberal Tradition in America: An Interpretation of American Political Thought since the Revolution.* New York, NY: Harcourt, Brace, World, 1955.

Harwood, John. "Poll Shows Division on Court Pick." *Wall Street Journal.* July 15, 2005.

Hawaii Property Owners Fighting Eminent Domain Abuse. *Amici Curiae to the United States Supreme Court in* Susette Kelo v. City of New London, 2004.

Hayek, F. A. The Road to Serfdom. Chicago, IL: University of Chicago Press, 1944.

Hearing before the Committee on the Judiciary on the United States. *The Kelo Decision: Investigating Takings of Homes and Other Private Property.* Senate Hearing 109–208. Washington, D.C.: U.S. Government Printing Office, September 20, 2005.

Hearing before the Subcommittee on Commerce, Trade, and Consumer Protection of the Committee on Energy and Commerce. House of Representatives. *Protecting Property Rights After* Kelo. Serial Number 109–55. Washington, D.C.: U.S. Government Printing Office, October 19, 2005.

Hogue, Arthur R. *Origins of the Common Law.* Reprint. Indianapolis, IN: Liberty Fund, Inc, 1986.

Holt, J.C. *Magna Carta.* 2nd ed. Cambridge, UK: Cambridge University Press, 1992.

Hume, David. *The History of England: From the Invasion of Julius Caesar to the Revolution in 1688.* Abridged with Introduction by Rodney W. Kilcup. Chicago, IL: University of Chicago Press, 1975.

Johnson, Simon, John McMillan, and Christopher Woodruff. "Property Rights and Finance." *The American Economic Review,* 92, no. 5 (December 2002): 1335–1356.

Karch, Andrew. "Emerging Issues and Future Directions in State Policy Diffusion Research." *State Politics and Policy Quarterly,* 7, no. 1 (Spring 2007): 54–80.

Kendall, Willmoore. *Willmoore Kendall: Contra Mundum.* ed., Nellie D. Kendall. Lanham, MD: University Press of America, 1971.

Kent, James. *Commentaries on American Law.* New York. 3rd ed., 1836.

Kollman, Ken. "Inviting Friends to Lobby: Interest Groups, Ideological Bias, and Congressional Committees." *American Journal of Political Science,* 41, no. 1 (April 1997): 519–545.

Kotlyarevskaya, Olga. "Public Use Requirement in Eminent Domain Cases Based on Slum Clearance, Elimination of Urban Blight, and Economic Development." *Connecticut Public Interest Law Journal,* 5, no. 2 (Spring 2006): 197–231.

La Porta, Rafael, Florencio Lopez-de-Silanes, Andrei Shleifer, and Robert W. Vishny. "Law and Finance." *Journal of Political Economy,* 106, no. 6 (1998): 1113–1155.

La Porta, Rafael, Florencio Lopez-de-Silanes, Andrei Shleifer, and Robert W. Vishny. "Legal Determinants of External Finance." *Journal of Finance.* 52, no. 3 (July 1997): 1131–1150.

Lee, Arthur. *An Appeal to the Justice and Interests of the People of Great Britain, in the Present Dispute with America.* 4th ed. New York, NY, 1775.

Levy, Leonard W. *Origins of the Bill of Rights.* New Haven, CT: Yale University Press, 1999.

Levy, Leonard W. *Seasoned Judgments.* New Brunswick, NJ: Transaction Publishers, 1995.

Levitt, Steven D. "How Do Senators Vote? Disentangling the Role of Voter Preferences, Party Affiliation, and Senator Ideology." *American Economic Review,* 86, no. 3 (June 1996): 425–441.

Lewis, Harold S., and Elizabeth J. Norman. *Civil Rights Law and Practice.* 2nd ed. St Paul, MN: Thomson/West, 2004.

Locke, John. *A Letter Concerning Toleration.* ed., Ian Shapiro. New Haven, CT: Yale University Press, 2003.

Locke, John. *Second Treatise of Government.* ed., C. B. Macpherson. Indianapolis, IN: Hackett Publishing Company, Inc, 1980.

Lutz, Donald S. 1984. "The Relative Influence of European Writers on Late Eighteenth-Century American Political Thought." *American Political Science Review,* 78, no. 1 (March 1984): 189–197.

Lyon, Bryce. *A Constitutional and Legal History of Medieval England.* New York, NY: W. W. Norton and Company, 1980.

Madison, James. *James Madison: Writings.* ed., Jack Rakove. New York, NY: Library of America, 1999.

Madison, James. *The Complete Madison.* ed., Saul Padover. New York, NY: Harper and Brothers, 1953.

McCarty, Nolan, Keith T. Poole, and Howard Rosenthal. "The Hunt for Party Discipline in Congress." *American Political Science Review,* 95, no. 3 (September 2001): 673–387.

McIlwain, Charles H. *Constitutionalism Ancient and Modern.* Ithaca, NY: Cornell University Press, 1947.

Meernik, James. 1995. "Congress, the President, and the Commitment of the U.S. Military." *Legislative Studies Quarterly,* 20, no. 1 (1995): 377–392.

Mintrom, Michael, and Sandra Vergari. "Policy Networks and Innovation Diffusion: The Case of State Educational Reform." *Journal of Politics,* 60, no. 1 (February 1998): 126–148.

National Association for the Advancement of Colored People. *Amici Curiae to the United States Supreme Court in* Susette Kelo v. City of New London, 2004.

New Jersey Property Owners Fighting Eminent Domain Abuse. *Amici Curiae to the United States Supreme Court in* Susette Kelo v. City of New London, 2004.

North, Douglass C. *Institutions, Institutional Change, and Economic Performance.* Cambridge, UK: Cambridge University Press, 1990.

North, Douglass C. *Structure and Change in Economic History.* New York, NY: W. W. Norton and Co, 1981.

North, Douglass C., and R. Thomas. 1971. "The Rise and Fall of the Manorial System: A Theoretical Model." *Journal of Economic History,* 31, no. 4 (December 1971): 777–803.

Ober, Josiah. "Natural Capacities and Democracy as a Good-in-Itself." *Philosophical Studies,* 132 (2006): 59–73.

O'Driscoll, Gerald P., and Lee Hoskins. "Property Rights: The Key to Economic Development." *Policy Analysis.* No. 482, (August 7, 2003): 1–27.

Palmer, Robert C. "Liberties as Constitutional Provisions." *Liberty and Community: Constitution and Rights in the Early American Republic.* New York: Oceana Publications, Inc, 1987.

Pangle, Thomas L. *The Spirit of Modern Republicanism: The Moral Vision of the American Founders and the Philosophy of Locke.* Chicago: IL: University of Chicago Press, 1988.

Pennsylvania Property Owners Fighting Eminent Domain Abuse. *Amici Curiae to the United States Supreme Court in* Susette Kelo v. City of New London, 2004.

Perry, Rick. Press Release, Governor Perry Signs New Law Protecting Property Rights. http://www.governor.state.tx.us/divisions/press/pressreleases/PressRelease .2005-08-31.3313, 2005.

Pipes, Richard. *Property and Freedom.* New York, NY: Alfred A. Knopf, 1999.

Pocock, J. G. A. *The Machiavellian Moment: Florentine Political Thought and the Atlantic Republican Tradition.* Princeton, NJ: Princeton University Press, 1975.

Postema, Gerald. "Classical Common Law Jurisprudence: Part II." *Oxford University Commonwealth Law Journal,* 3, no.1 (Summer 2003): 1–28.

Postema, Gerald. "Classical Common Law Jurisprudence: Part I." *Oxford University Commonwealth Law Journal,* 2 (Autumn 2002): 155–180.

Reinsch, Paul Samuel. *English Common Law in the Early American Colonies.* New York, NY: Da Capo Press, 1970.

Rell, M. Jodi. Statement of Governor Rell on Call for Legislative Hearings on Eminent Domain, Press Release, July, 11, 2005.

Rutledge, John. *The First American Constitutions: Republican Ideology and the Making of State Constitutions in the Revolutionary Era.* ed., Willi Paul Adams. Chapel Hill, NC: University of North Carolina Press, 1980.

Sabine, George. *A History of Political Theory.* 3rd ed. New York, NY: Holt, Rinehart, and Winston, 1961.

Sandefur, Timothy. *Cornerstone of Liberty: Property Rights in 21st-Century America.* Washington, D.C.: Cato Institute, 2006.

Schwartz, Bernard. *The Bill of Rights: A Documentary History.* 2 Vols. New York, NY: McGraw Hill Book Co, 1971.

Scott, Kyle. *Dismantling American Common Law: Liberty and Justice in Our Transformed Courts.* Lanham, MD: Lexington Books, 2008.

Siegan, Bernard. *Property Rights: From Magna Carta to the Fourteenth Amendment.* New Brunswick, NJ: Transaction Publishers, 2001.

Siegan, Bernard. *Property and Freedom: The Constitution, the Courts, and Land-Use Regulation.* New Brunswick, NJ: Transaction Publishers, 1997.

Smith, Richard A. "Interest Group Influence in the U.S. Congress." *Legislative Studies Quarterly,* 20, no. 1 (1995): 89.

Snyder, James M. Jr., and Tim Groseclose. "Estimating Party Influence on Roll Call Voting: Regression Coefficients versus Classification Success." *American Political Science Review,* 95, no. 3 (September 2001): 689–698.

Sommerville, J. P. *Royalists and Patriots: Politics and Ideology in England, 1603–1640.* New York, NY: Addison-Wesley Longman, 1999.

Stoner, James R. *Common Law and Liberal Theory: Coke, Hobbes, and the Origins of Constitutionalism.* Lawrence, KS: University Press of Kansas, 1992.

Story, Joseph. *Commentaries on the Constitution,* 1833.

Stratmann, Thomas. 2000. "Congressional Voting over Legislative Careers: Shifting Positions and Changing Constraints." *American Political Science Review,* 94, no. 3 (September 2000): 665–676.

Strauss, Leo. *Natural Right and History.* Chicago, IL: University of Chicago Press, 1953.

Sunstein, Cass R. *Radicals in Robes: Why Extreme Right-Wing Courts Are Wrong for America.* New York, NY: Basic Books, 2005.

Tansill, Charles Callan. ed. "Declaration and Resolves of the First Continental Congress, October 14, 1774." Reprinted in *Making of the American Republic: The Great Documents 1774–1789.* Arlington, VA: Arlington House, 1972.

Texas Property Owners Fighting Eminent Domain Abuse. *Amici Curiae to the United States Supreme Court in* Susette Kelo v. City of New London, 2004.

Thomas, Clive S., and Ronald J. Hrebenar. "Changing Patterns of Interest Group Activity: A Regional Perspective." In *The Politics of Interests: Interest Groups Transformed,* ed., Mark P. Petracca. Boulder, CO: Westview Press, 1992.

Tocqueville, Alexis. *Democracy in America.* J. P. Mayer and trans., George Lawrence. New York, NY: Harper Perennial, 1969.

Trenchard, John. "*Cato no. 68.*" in *Founder's Constitution.* Vol. I. eds., Philip Kurland and Ralph Lerner, eds. Indianapolis, IN: Liberty Fund, Inc, 1987.

Tully, James. *A Discourse on Property.* Cambridge, UK: Cambridge University Press, 1980.

Vance, Laurence M. 2007. "The *Kelo* Decision and the Fourteenth Amendment." *Journal of Libertarian Studies,* 21, no. 2 (Summer 2007): 69–100.

Wiggins, Charles W., Keith E. Hamm, and Charles G. Bell. "Interest-Group and Party Influence Agents in the Legislative Process: A Comparative State Analysis." *Journal of Politics,* 54, no. 1 (February 1992): 82–100.

Zuckert, Michael P. "Social Compact, Common Law, and the American Amalgam: The Contribution of William Blackstone." in *The American Founding and the Social Compact.* ed., Ronald J. Pestritto and Thomas G. West. Lanham, MD: Lexington Books, 2003.

Zuckert, Michael P. *Launching Liberalism: On Lockean Political Philosophy.* Lawrence, KS: University Press of Kansas, 2002.

Zuckert, Michael P. *Natural Rights and the New Republicanism.* Princeton, NJ: Princeton University Press, 1994.

Index

Ackerman, Bruce, xii
acquisition: by community, 37; money enabling, 36–37; of property, 34–35, 37–38; rights and, 35–36
Adams, Willi Paul, 65–66
Agins v. Tiburon, 90
agriculture, 124
Alschuler, Albert, 23
American Farm Bureau Federation, 119
American Revolution, 7
Articles of Confederation, 68
artificial reason: of common law, 13–14; components of, 14
autonomy, of jurists, 21

Barron v. Baltimore, 110
BEA. *See* Bureau of Economic Analysis
Berman v. Parker, 100
Besley, Timothy, 134–35
Bill of Rights, xiii, 7, 28, 63; Magna Carta and, 29; property as term in, 72, 82–83; ratification, xvi, 17, 68–71, 84
Blackstone, William, 1, 120; Coke v., 17; on common law, 17–26; as common law thinker, 28; first principles implemented by, 18–20; on natural law, 19–20; on precedent, 20; on

property rights, 24–25, 31n10; on scientific reasoning, 18; on self-love, 18
Boston Tea Party, xi
Bureau of Economic Analysis (BEA), 140

Calder v. Bull, 104
Carolene Products, 104
Case of the Isle of Ely, 15
Case of the King's Prerogative in Saltpeter, 14–15
Cato's Letters (Trenchard), 115
Chase, Samuel, 104
Church, ownership claims of, 2
Claesens, Stijin, 134
Coke, Edward, 1, 6; American colonists on, 16; Blackstone v., 17; cases heard by, 14–15; on due process, 8–9; as embodiment of common law, 16–17; on judiciary's role, 10–11; legal reasoning of, 120; on Magna Carta, 8–9; property's importance in writing of, 16
Cole v. La Grange, 101
common law, 132n11; in American psyche, 26; artificial reason of, 13–14; Blackstone on, 17–26, 28;